THE UNQUENCHABLE FLAME

Discovering the heart of the Reformation

REFORMATION
500
EDITION

D1354686

MICHAEL REEVES

Foreword by Mark Dever

ivp

The Reformation was about how Christ loves his Spouse.
This book is written with such love to mine.
To Bethan

INTER-VARSITY PRESS
36 Causton Street, London SW1P 4ST, England
Email: ivp@ivpbooks.com
Website: www.ivpbooks.com

First published 2009
Reprinted 2010, 2011, 2012, 2013, 2014, 2015, 2016
Reissued with Foreword 2016

British Library Cataloguing-in-Publication Data
A catalogue record for this book is available from the British Library

ISBN: 978-1-78359-529-7
eBook ISBN: 978-1-78359-530-3

Set in Dante 11.5/14pt
Typeset in Great Britain by CRB Associates, Potterhanworth, Lincolnshire
Printed and bound in Great Britain by Ashford Colour Press Ltd, Gosport, Hampshire

Inter-Varsity Press publishes Christian books that are true to the Bible and that communicate the gospel, develop discipleship and strengthen the church for its mission in the world.

IVP originated within the Inter-Varsity Fellowship, now the Universities and Colleges Christian Fellowship, a student movement connecting Christian Unions in universities and colleges throughout Great Britain, and a member movement of the International Fellowship of Evangelical Students. Website: www.uccf.org.uk. That historic association is maintained, and all senior IVP staff and committee members subscribe to the UCCF Basis of Faith.

Contents

Map of key places in the Reformation   4

Foreword by Mark Dever   5

Prologue: Here I stand   7

1 **Going medieval on religion**   10
   The background to the Reformation

2 **God's volcano**   30
   Martin Luther

3 **Soldiers, sausages and revolution**   61
   Ulrich Zwingli and the Radical Reformers

4 **After darkness, light**   87
   John Calvin

5 **Burning passion**   115
   The Reformation in Britain

6 **Reforming the Reformation**   144
   The Puritans

7 **Is the Reformation over?**   171

   Reformation timeline   186

   Further reading   189

Key places in the Reformation

Foreword

This is a story that needs to be told again today and Michael Reeves has done a significant service to us in doing exactly that.

Five hundred years ago, the Roman Catholic Church warned the Protestant reformers and those who were tempted to follow them that their movement would divide and dissolve into countless factions if they rejected the authority of the Bishop of Rome. The years of conflict turned into decades and they, in turn, receded into centuries of separation from Rome. Now, half a millennium in, it can conclusively be said that Rome's fears of infinite instability and division were unfounded.

The authority of the Bible has ensured that millions upon millions of Protestants have believed and shared the same gospel for centuries. An Assembly of God missionary in the Philippines, an Anglican minister in Sydney or Tanzania, a Baptist pastor in Brazil, a Lutheran minister in St Louis, a Presbyterian minister in Scotland, a Korean missionary in Stockholm or an interdenominational pastor in Dubai may never have met. They may never be a part of the same earthly organization, but, unlike what Rome feared would happen, they are now, and will remain, united in the gospel of Jesus Christ.

This book focuses on the first few decades of a remarkable time in the church. With stories, anecdotes and explanations that catch something of the flash and thunder of the insights and conflicts that occurred, it tells of the attempted reform of the universal church and its rejection by many of those in positions of power and authority.

For the past several decades, it has been the accepted thing to tell the story of the Reformation from Rome's standpoint. To many, 'the Protestant Reformation' has been removed from history altogether, thought of as little more than pious propaganda, more hagiography than history. The Roman Catholic Church itself has worked officially to bring about a rapprochement with Protestants via the Joint Declaration on the Doctrine of Justification (1999).

With the skill of a scholar and the art of a storyteller, Michael Reeves sets the record straight and has written what is, quite simply, the best brief introduction to the Reformation I have read. If you've been looking for a book to understand the Reformation or just to begin to study church history, this little volume brings that history to life. The only other title that I can think to compare this with, which you may want to read after this one, is Roland Bainton's *Here I Stand: A Life of Martin Luther* (Signet, 1955). Like Bainton, Reeves gives the reader serious scholarship in lively prose. Scenes are carefully chosen and theological controversies judiciously weighed and recounted.

Characters and their theology are recounted with historical accuracy and theological precision, even as the story is told with clarity, boldness, humour and an engaging earnestness. Confident that you will be informed, prayerful that you will be edified, I invite you to read and come to know the rest of the story.

Mark Dever
President, 9 Marks and
Senior Pastor, Capitol Hill Baptist Church
Washington, DC

Prologue: Here I stand

The trumpets blared as the covered wagon passed through the city gate. Thousands lined the streets to catch a glimpse of their hero, many more waving pictures of him from windows and rooftops. It was the evening of Wednesday 16 April 1521, and Martin Luther was entering the city of Worms.

It looked like a triumphal entry. Yet Luther knew where triumphal entries could lead. The reality was, he was coming to be tried for his life, and, like Jesus, he was expecting death. Teaching that a sinner, merely by trusting Christ, could, despite all his or her sins, have utter confidence before God, he had brought down on himself the fury of the church. His books had already been thrown onto bonfires, and most expected that in a few days he would be joining them. Luther, however, was determined to defend his teaching: 'Christ lives,' he said, 'and we shall enter Worms in spite of all the gates of hell.'

The next day, the imperial herald came to Luther's lodging to escort him to the trial. The crowds were so dense that he was forced to sneak Luther through some back alleys to the bishop's palace. Even so, they did not go unnoticed, many scrambling over the rooftops in their eagerness to see. At four in the afternoon, Luther entered the hall; and for the first time the miner's son from Saxony, dressed in his humble monk's habit, faced

Worms in the sixteenth century

Charles V, the Holy Roman Emperor, lord of Spain, Austria, Burgundy, southern and northern Italy, the Netherlands, and 'God's Viceroy on earth'. On seeing the monk, the emperor, a fierce defender of the church, mumbled 'He will not make a heretic out of me'.

Luther was ordered not to speak until bidden. Then the emperor's spokesman, pointing at a pile of Luther's books on a table in front of him, told him that he had been summoned to see whether he would acknowledge the books that had been published in his name, and if so, whether he would recant. In a soft voice that people strained to hear, Luther admitted that the books were his. But then, to the shock of all, he asked for more time to decide whether he needed to recant. It looked like he was going to back down. In fact, Luther had been expecting to deal with specific things he had taught; he had not anticipated that he might be asked to reject everything he had ever written. That needed further consideration. He was grudgingly given one day to reflect, and after that, he was warned, he should expect the worst if he did not repent.

The following day, it was six in the evening before Luther was readmitted into the emperor's presence. The hall was packed, and in the gathering gloom torches had been lit, making it stiflingly hot. As a result, Luther was perspiring heavily. Looking at him, everyone expected an abject apology as he begged forgiveness for his heinous heresy. But the moment he opened his mouth it was clear that was not to be. This time he spoke in a loud and ringing voice. He announced that he could not retract his attacks upon false teaching, for that would give even more rein to those who thus destroyed Christianity. 'Good God, what sort of tool of evil and tyranny I then would be!' Despite an angry shout of 'No!' from the emperor, Luther went on, demanding that, if he be wrong, he be refuted with Scripture; then, he promised, he would be the first to burn his books.

For the last time he was asked if he would retract his errors, and then he concluded:

> I am bound by the Scriptures I have quoted and my conscience is captive to the Word of God. I cannot and I will not retract anything, since it is neither safe nor right to go against conscience. I cannot do otherwise, here I stand, may God help me, Amen.

It was no mere bluster. For Luther, it was the word of God that had freed him and saved him. He had no other security. But with it he had the courage to stand when the emperor's spokesman responded by blasting him with his arrogance for believing he was the only one to know the truth. Indeed, at that point he did seem to be standing against the whole world.

Two soldiers then escorted Luther from the hall, amid shouts of 'To the pyre with him!' A large crowd followed them to his quarters. When he got there, he raised his hands, smiled and shouted 'I've come through! I've come through!'; then, turning to a friend, he told him that, even if he had a thousand heads, he would rather have them all lopped off than abandon his gospel.

Back in the hall, the emperor declared that one monk who stood against all Christendom had to be wrong, and therefore he had determined 'to stake on this cause my kingdoms and seignories, my friends, my body and blood, my life and soul'. The lines were drawn. The Reformation had begun. And that evening, Luther had done more than write a page of history; he had thrown out a challenge for every generation.

1 Going medieval on religion:
the background to the Reformation

As the fifteenth century died and the sixteenth was born, the old world seemed to die at the hands of a new one: the mighty Byzantine Empire, last remnant of Imperial Rome, had collapsed; then Columbus discovered a new world in the Americas, Copernicus turned the universe on its head with his heliocentrism, and Luther literally re-formed Christianity. All the old foundations that once had seemed so solid and certain now crumbled in this storm of change, making way for a new era in which things would be very different.

Looking back today, it feels nigh on impossible even to get a sense of what it must have been like in that era. 'Medieval' – the very word conjures up dark, gothic images of chanting cloister-crazed monks and superstitious, revolting peasants. All very strange. Especially to modern eyes: where we are out-and-out democratic egalitarians, they saw everything hierarchically; where our lives revolve around nurturing, nourishing and pampering the self, they sought in everything to abolish and abase the self (or, at least, they admired those who did). The list of differences could go on. Yet this was the setting for the Reformation, the context for why people got so passionate about theology. The Reformation was a revolution, and revolutions not only fight for something, they also fight against something, in this case, the old world of medieval Roman Catholicism. What, then, was it like to be a Christian in the couple of centuries before the Reformation?

Popes, priests and purgatory

Unsurprisingly, all the roads of medieval Roman Catholicism led to Rome. The apostle Peter, to whom Jesus had said 'You are Peter, and upon this rock I will build my church', was thought to have been martyred and buried there, allowing the church to be built, quite literally, upon him. And so, as once the Roman Empire had looked to Rome as its mother and Caesar as its father, now the Christian empire of the Church looked still to Rome as its mother, and to Peter's successor as father, 'papa' or 'pope'. There was a slightly awkward exception to this: the Eastern Orthodox Church, severed from the Church of Rome since the eleventh century. But every family has a black sheep. Other than that, all Christians recognized Rome and the pope as their irreplaceable parents. Without Father Pope there

A papal procession

could be no Church; without Mother Church there could be no salvation.

The pope was held to be Christ's 'vicar' (representative) on earth, and as such, he was the channel through whom all of God's grace flowed. He had the power to ordain bishops, who in turn could ordain priests; and together, they, the clergy, were the ones with the authority to turn on the taps of grace. Those taps were the seven sacraments: baptism, confirmation, the Mass, penance, marriage, ordination and last rites. Sometimes they were spoken of as the seven arteries of the Body of Christ, through which the lifeblood of God's grace was pumped. That this all looks rather mechanistic was precisely the point, for the unwashed masses, being uneducated and illiterate, were considered incapable of having an explicit faith. So, while an 'explicit faith' was considered desirable, an 'implicit faith', in which a person came along to church and received the sacraments, was considered perfectly acceptable. If they stood under the taps they received the grace.

It was through baptism that people (generally as infants) were first admitted to the Church to taste God's grace. Yet it was the Mass that was really central to the whole system. That would be made obvious the moment you walked into your local church: all the architecture led towards the altar, on which the Mass would be celebrated. And it was called an altar with good reason, for in the Mass Christ's body would be sacrificed afresh to God. It was through this 'unbloody' sacrifice offered day after day, repeating Christ's 'bloody' sacrifice on the cross, that God's anger at sin would be appeased. Each day Christ would be re-offered to God as an atoning sacrifice. Thus the sins of each day were dealt with.

Yet wasn't it obvious that something was missing from this sacrifice, that Christ's body wasn't actually on the altar, that the priest was only handling mere bread and wine? This was the genius of the doctrine of transubstantiation. According to Aristotle, each thing has its own 'substance' (inner reality) as well as 'accidents' (appearance). The 'substance' of a chair, for instance, could be wood, while its 'accidents' are brownness and dirtiness. Paint the chair and its 'accidents' would change. Transubstantiation imagined the opposite: the 'substance' of the bread and wine would, in the Mass, be transformed into the literal body and blood of Christ, whilst the original 'accidents' of bread and wine remained. It may all have seemed a bit far-fetched, but there were enough stories doing the rounds to persuade doubters, stories of people having visions of real blood in the chalice, real flesh on the plate and so on.

The moment of transformation came when the priest spoke Christ's words in Latin *Hoc est corpus meum* ('this is my body'). Then the church bells would peal and the priest would raise the bread. The people would normally only get to eat the bread once a year (and they never got to drink from the cup – after all, what if some ham-fisted peasant spilt the blood of Christ on the floor?), but grace came with just a look at the raised bread. It was under-standable that the more devoted should run feverishly from church to church to see more masses and thus receive more grace.

The service of the Mass was said in Latin. The people, of course, understood not a word. The trouble was, neither did many of the clergy, who found learning the service by rote quicker than learning a whole new language. Thus when parishioners heard 'Hocus pocus' instead of *Hoc est corpus meum*, who knows whose mistake it was? Even priests were known to fluff their lines. And with little understanding of what was being said, it was hard for the average parishioner to distinguish Roman Catholic ortho-doxy from magic and superstition. For them the consecrated bread became a talisman of divine power that could be carried around to avert accidents, given to sick animals as a medicine or planted to encourage a good harvest. Much of the time the Church was lenient towards semi-pagan folk Christianity, but it is a testimony to how highly the Mass was revered that it decided to act against such abuses: in 1215, the fourth Lateran Council ordered that the transformed bread and wine 'are to be kept locked away in a safe place in all churches, so that no audacious hand can reach them to do anything horrible or impious'.

Underpinning the whole system and mentality of medieval Roman Catholicism was an understanding of salvation that went back to Augustine (AD 354–430); Augustine's theology of love, to be precise (how ironic that this theology of love would come to inspire great fear). Augustine taught that we exist in order to love God. However, we cannot naturally do so, but must pray for God to help us. This he does by 'justifying' us, which, Augustine said, is the act in which God pours his love into our hearts (Romans 5:5). This is the effect of the grace that God was said to channel through the sacraments: by making us more and more loving, more and more just, God 'justifies' us. God's grace, on this model, was the fuel needed to become a better, more just, righteous and loving person. And this was the sort of person who finally merited salvation, according to Augustine. This was what Augustine had meant when he spoke of salvation by grace.

Talk of God pouring out his grace so that we become loving and so merit salvation might have sounded lovely on Augustine's lips; over the centuries, however, such thoughts took on a darker hue. Nobody intended it. Quite the opposite: how God's grace worked was still spoken of in attractive, optimistic ways. 'God will not deny grace to those who do their best' was the cheery slogan on the lips of medieval theologians. But then, how could you be sure you really had done your best? How could you tell if you had become the sort of just person who merited salvation?

In 1215, the fourth Lateran Council came up with what it hoped would be a useful aid for all those seeking to be 'justified': it required all Christians (on pain of eternal damnation) to confess their sins regularly to a priest. There the conscience could be probed for sins and evil thoughts so that wickedness could be rooted out and the Christian become more just. The effect of the exercise, however, was far from reassuring to those who took it seriously. Using a long official list, the priest would ask questions such as: 'Are your prayers, alms and religious activities done more to hide your sins and impress others than to please God?' 'Have you loved relatives, friends or other creatures more than God?' 'Have you muttered against God because of bad weather, illness, poverty, the death of a child or a friend?' By the end it had been made very clear that one was not righteous and loving at all, but a mass of dark desires.

The effect was profoundly disturbing, as we can see in the fifteenth-century autobiography of Margery Kempe, a woman of Norfolk. She describes how she left one confession so terrified of the damnation that such a sinner as she surely deserved that she began to see devils surrounding her, pawing at her, making her bite and scratch herself. It is tempting for the modern mind quickly to ascribe this to some form of mental instability. Margery herself, however, is quite clear that her emotional meltdown was due simply to taking the theology of the day seriously. She knew from the confession that she was not righteous enough to have merited salvation.

Of course, the Church's official teaching was quite clear that nobody would die righteous enough to have merited salvation fully. But that was no cause for great alarm, for there was always purgatory. Unless Christians died unrepentant of a mortal sin such as murder (in which case they would go to hell), they would have the chance after death to have all their sins slowly purged from them in purgatory before entering heaven, fully cleansed. Around the end of the fifteenth century, Catherine of Genoa wrote a *Treatise on Purgatory* in which she described it in glowing

One of the torments of purgatory

terms. There, she explained, the souls relish and embrace their chastisements because of their desire to be purged and purified for God. More worldly souls than Catherine's, however, tended to be less upbeat about the prospect of thousands or millions of years of punishment. Instead of enjoying the prospect, most people sought to fast-track the route through purgatory, both for themselves, and for those they loved. As well as prayers, masses could be said for souls in purgatory, in which the grace of that Mass could be applied directly to the departed and tormented soul. An entire purgatory industry evolved for exactly this reason: the wealthy founded chantries (chapels with priests dedicated to saying prayers and masses for the soul of their sponsor or his fortunate beneficiaries); the less wealthy clubbed together in fraternities to pay for the same.

Robert Grosseteste (1168–1253)
Not everyone was prepared to toe the official line unquestioningly, of course. To take just one example, Robert Grosseteste, who became bishop of Lincoln in 1235, believed that the clergy should first and foremost be about preaching the Bible, not giving Mass. He himself rather unusually preached in English, rather than Latin, so that he might be understood by the people. He clashed a number of times with the pope (when, for example, a non-English-speaking priest was appointed to his diocese), going so far as to call the pope an antichrist who would be damned for his sin. Few could get away with such language, but Grosseteste was so famous, not only for his personal holiness, but as a scholar, scientist and linguist, that the pope felt unable to silence him.

Another aspect of medieval Roman Catholicism that was impossible to ignore was the cult of the saints. Europe was filled with shrines to various saints, and they were important, not just spiritually, but economically. With enough decent relics of its patron saint, a shrine could ensure a steady stream of pilgrims, making everyone a winner, from the pilgrims to the publicans. As much as anything, what seemed to fuel the cult was the way in which Christ became an increasingly daunting figure in the public mind through the Middle Ages. More and more, the risen and ascended Christ was seen as the Doomsday Judge, all-terrible in his holiness. Who could approach him? Surely he'd listen to his mother. And so, as Christ receded into heaven, Mary became the mediator through whom people could approach him. Yet, having been accorded such glory, Mary in turn became the inapproachable star-flaming Queen of Heaven. Using the same logic, people began to appeal to her mother, Anne, to intercede with her. And so the cult of St Anne grew, attracting the fervent devotion of many, including an obscure German family called the Luthers. It wasn't just St Anne; heaven was crammed with saints, all very suitable mediators between the sinful

Mary as Queen of Heaven, woodcut by Albrecht Dürer, 1511

and the Judge. And the earth seemed full of their relics, objects that could bestow some of their grace and merit. Of course, the authenticity of some of these relics was questionable: it was a standing joke that there were so many 'pieces of the true cross' spread across Christendom that the original cross itself must have been far too huge for a man to lift. But then, Christ was omnipotent.

The official line was that Mary and the saints were to be venerated, not worshipped; but on the ground that was much too subtle a distinction for people who were not being taught. All too often the army of saints was treated as a pantheon of gods, and their relics treated as magical talismans of power. Yet how could the illiterate be taught the complexities of this system of theology, and so avoid the sin of idolatry? The stock answer was that, even in the poorest churches, they were surrounded by pictures and images of saints and the Virgin Mary, in stained glass, in statues, in frescoes: these were 'the Bible of the poor', the 'books of the illiterate'. Lacking words, the people learnt from pictures. It has to be said, however, that the argument is a bit hollow: a statue of the Virgin Mary was hardly capable of teaching the distinction between veneration and worship. The very fact that services were in Latin, a language the people did not know, betrays the reality that teaching was not really a priority. Some theologians tried to get around this by arguing that Latin, as a holy language, was so powerful it could even affect those who did not understand it. It sounds rather unlikely. Rather, the fact was that people did not need to understand in order to receive God's grace. An unformed 'implicit faith' would do. Indeed, given the absence of teaching, it would have to.

Dynamic or diseased?

If ever you should be so unfortunate as to find yourself in a roomful of Reformation historians, the thing to do to generate some excitement is to ask loudly: 'Was Christianity on the eve of the Reformation vigorous or corrupt?' It is *the* question guaranteed to start a bun-fight. A few years ago it would hardly have caused a murmur; everyone then seemed happily agreed that before the Reformation the people of Europe were groaning for change, hating the oppressive yoke of the corrupt Roman Church. Now that view will not wash.

Historical research, especially from the 1980s and on, has shown beyond any doubt that in the generation before the Reformation, religion became more popular than ever. Certainly people had their grumbles, but the vast majority clearly threw themselves into it with gusto. More masses for the dead were paid for, more churches were built, more statues of saints were erected and more pilgrimages were made than ever before. Books of devotion and spirituality – as mixed in content as they are today – were extraordinarily popular among those who could read.

And, the religious zeal of the people meant that they were eager for reform. Throughout the fourteenth century, monastic orders were reforming themselves, and even the papacy underwent some piecemeal attempts at reform. Everyone agreed that there were a few dead branches and a few rotten apples on the tree of the Church. Everyone could laugh when the poet Dante placed Popes Nicholas III and Boniface VIII in the eighth circle of hell in his *Divine Comedy*. Of course there were corrupt old popes and priests who drank too much before Mass. But the very fact that people could laugh shows how solid and secure the Church appeared. It looked like it could take it. And the fact that they wanted to prune the dead wood only shows how they loved the tree. Such desires for reform never came close to imagining that there might be fatal rot in the trunk of the tree. After all, wanting better popes is something very different from wanting no popes; wanting better priests and masses very different to wanting no separate priesthood and no masses. And this Dante also showed: not only did he punish bad popes in his *Inferno*, he also meted out divine vengeance on those who opposed popes, for popes, good or bad, were, after all, the vicars of Christ. Such were most Christians on the eve of the Reformation: devoted, and devoted to the improvement, but not the overthrow, of their religion. This was not a society looking for radical change, only a clearing-up of acknowledged abuses.

So, vigorous or corrupt? It is a false antithesis. Christianity on the eve of the Reformation was undoubtedly popular and lively, but that does not mean it was healthy or biblical. In fact, if all the people had been hungering for the kind of change the Reformation would bring, it would suggest that the Reformation was little more than a natural social movement, a moral clean-up. This the Reformers always denied. It was not a popular moral reform; it was a challenge to the very heart of Christianity. They claimed that God's word was breaking in to change the world; it was unexpected, and went right against the grain; it was not a human work but a divine bombshell.

Omens of apocalypse

The Reformation might have been unlooked-for, the majority contenting themselves with small-scale reform, and yet in the sunny medieval sky dark clouds began to form. They were at first but the size of a man's hand. Nobody knew it, but they were portents that the heavens were about to fall on medieval Roman Catholicism.

The first formed right over Rome itself. In 1305 the Archbishop of Bordeaux was elected pope. However, for various reasons he was not interested in relocating to Rome, as expected of popes, but instead made Avignon in the south of France his new papal headquarters. The king of France was delighted: a French pope on French turf would be so much easier to do business with. And so, nobody was very surprised when the next pope to be elected was also French, and also chose to stay in Avignon. And thus things were with the next few popes. Outside of France, people were less thrilled. The 'Babylonian Captivity of the Church' they called it. The pope was supposed to be the bishop of Rome, the mother church; but were these men in Avignon really bishops of Rome? And so Christendom began to lose confidence in the papacy.

After seventy years the people of Rome were fed up; the papal court, after all, had been their city's greatest source of dignity (and revenue). Thus in 1378, when the College of Cardinals sat in Rome to elect the next pope, a mob besieged them, demanding the election of a proper Italian, and preferably Roman, pope. The terrified cardinals understandably gave in to the mob's demands. They soon began to regret their decision, however, when they saw how domineering and aggressive the new pope was. Many started voicing the opinion that the election could not have been valid, given that it had been conducted under duress. And so they elected a new pope, a Frenchman. Unfortunately, the first appointee, still in perfect health, refused to stand down, meaning that there were now two popes, who naturally excommunicated each other. Effectively, with two Holy Fathers, this entailed that there were now two Mother Churches.

All Europe was divided in its allegiance. France, of course, supported the French pope, so instinctively England supported the other, and so on. The situation was unsustainable, and so a council was called to end the problem. Its solution was to depose both existing popes and elect a new one. Inevitably, though, neither existing pope would go so easily. And so then there were three. The 'Great Schism', as it was called, was only ended by a more robust council, the Council of Constance, which met from 1414–18. This council managed to get two of the popes to agree to resign, and the third pope in Avignon, who refused, they declared deposed. In their place they elected a new pope, and apart from a tiny remnant of supporters for the Avignon pope, everybody accepted this one. The schism was over, but it had created a crisis of authority: where was the supreme authority in the Church? In Avignon or Rome? And since a council had established which pope was pope, was a council an authority superior to the pope? The crisis of authority was to linger long after the schism was over, for while the Council of Constance had declared that a council was superior in authority to the pope, the popes fought tooth and nail against the idea. With so many competing contenders, how could the ordinary Christian know God's will?

In the meantime, with the popes elsewhere, the city of Rome had fallen into decay. It was more than a shame, for if Rome was to be the glorious mother to which all Christendom looked, she could not be a ruin. Indeed, to recover her status, she needed to be made more glorious than ever. All Europe needed to be dazzled. Over the next century, then, the Renaissance popes pulled a galaxy of stars into their orbit: Fra Angelico, Gozzoli and Pinturrichio were all employed; Raphael was commissioned to decorate the pope's personal apartments in the Vatican; Michelangelo to adorn the Sistine Chapel; Bramante to rebuild

St Peter's Basilica. Glorious it may have been; it was also hide-
ously expensive. Funding was sought wherever it could be found,
and people began to grumble at popes who seemed more interested in their money than their souls, and for art that looked to
them more pagan than Christian. The rebuilding of St Peter's,
especially, would prove more costly to Rome than a pope's worst
nightmare, for it would rouse the wrath of Martin Luther.

Rome in 1493

There also began to be an air of sleaze about the place, which,
coupled with the glitz, made Rome the Las Vegas of its day.
Especially under the Borgias. In 1492 Rodrigo Borgia took the
simple but effective step of buying the necessary votes to get
himself elected as Pope Alexander VI. It was an appropriate start
to a reign to make a cardinal blush. He had numerous children
by his mistresses, he was rumoured to have had another with his
party-throwing, poison-ring-wearing daughter Lucrezia, and is
best remembered for his habit of throwing orgies in the Vatican
and poisoning his cardinals. It did not set a good precedent
for the office of the Holy Father: his successor, the war-loving
Julius II, was also 'papa' in more senses than one, and Julius'
successor, Leo X, was an agnostic (ordained at the age of seven,
nobody had thought to ask). Of course the papacy had had its
low points before, but in the midst of the Church's crisis of
authority, it was a bad time for it to lose its respectability.

Morning stars of the Reformation

The second cloud in the otherwise clear medieval sky started gathering in northern England, over Yorkshire. It was caused by the birth there, sometime in the 1320s, of John Wycliffe. He was ordained as a priest and moved to Oxford, where his theological views made him the university's most controversial figure, and his connections to the royal family made him influential. For almost all of Wycliffe's life, the popes resided in Avignon, and thus he grew up in an atmosphere in which religious authority was constantly being questioned. But with the inauguration of two popes in 1378, Wycliffe began publicly to identify the Bible, and not the pope, as the supreme source of spiritual authority. The papacy, he argued, was merely a human invention, whereas the Bible authoritatively determined the validity of all religious beliefs and practices. On this basis he rejected the highly philosophical doctrine of transubstantiation.

In a few short years such talk had got Oxford – and the whole country – seething. Wycliffe had to retire, which he did, to the obscure parish of Lutterworth in Leicestershire, where he lived out the last few years of his life as the parish priest. He was not idle in that time, however: he wrote popular tracts explaining his views, commissioned preachers, and organized a translation of the Latin Vulgate Bible into English. Fortunately for Wycliffe, he died in 1384 before the Council of Constance

Wycliffe's bones being burned

condemned him as a heretic (whereupon his remains were exhumed, burned, and scattered); yet his legacy was great. With a Bible in English in their hands, his followers in England dedicated themselves to the illegal practice of secret group Bible reading. It was most likely for this reason that they were known as 'Lollards', a term that probably meant 'mumbler', in reference to their habit of secretly reading out the Bible. They would be a highly receptive audience for the Reformation when it arrived a century later.

Indulgences

In medieval Roman Catholicism, when a sinner went to confess to a priest, the priest would demand that various acts of penance be performed. Any sins for which penance had not been performed in this life would have to be dealt with in purgatory. The good news was that there were saints who had been so good that, not only had they had enough merit to enter heaven direct, bypassing purgatory altogether, they had actually had more merit than they needed to get into heaven. This spare merit of theirs was kept, as it were, in the church's treasury, to which only the pope had the keys. The pope could therefore give a gift of merit (an indulgence) to any soul he deemed worthy, fast-tracking that soul's path through purgatory, or even leap-frogging purgatory all together (with a 'full', or 'plenary' indulgence). Initially, these full indulgences were offered for participation in the First Crusade, but soon a gift of money was deemed penitential enough to merit an indulgence. It became increasingly clear in people's minds: a bit of cash could secure spiritual bliss.

Perhaps more important than the Lollards for Wycliffe's legacy, were those visiting students at Oxford who took his teachings back home with them to Bohemia (in the modern-day Czech Republic). There, Wycliffe's ideas were warmly received by many, including the rector of the University of Prague, Jan Hus. Hus did not quite have Wycliffe's penetrating intellect, but he came to be at least as significant by playing the role of Wycliffe's bulldog. When attempts were made to stamp out Wycliffe's teachings in

Bohemia, Hus defended him, and became increasingly outspoken in his critiques of the Church, to the point where he publicly denied the power of popes to issue indulgences and expressed doubts about the existence of purgatory.

Hus was excommunicated, and summoned to the Council of Constance to defend his views. Unsurprisingly he was rather reluctant to risk being burnt as a heretic by walking so easily into the lions' den, but then he was given a guarantee of safe conduct, and so he went. The guarantee amounted to nothing, however; he was immediately imprisoned, and after six months in prison and a mock trial in which he refused to recant his views he was summarily condemned to death for heresy in 1415.

Jan Hus

His death sparked off an armed revolt by his followers in Bohemia, where he had become something of a national hero. And when, from 1420, a series of crusades were launched against what Catholic Europe saw as the heretical Hussites, amazingly the Hussites won, allowing them to establish an independent Hussite church in the very heart of Catholic Europe. There, free from papal control, Hussite preachers were allowed to speak the word of God freely, and the Hussites received both bread and wine in Communion, rather than the Catholic Mass. As well as leaving this sizeable thorn in Rome's flesh, shortly before he died, Hus is said to have uttered the words 'You may roast this goose ['Hus' means 'goose' in Czech], but a hundred years from now a swan will arise whose singing you will not be able to silence'. Almost exactly a hundred years later, Martin Luther unleashed the doctrine of justification by faith alone on the world. A great admirer of Hus, Luther was ardent in his belief that he was the promised swan; after his death, Lutheran churches would use swans as weather vanes, and the Reformer would often be portrayed with a swan. The base of the great statue of Hus in Prague reads 'Great is the truth, and it prevails'; certainly, Hus and his message had a future.

Books, dangerous books

The other main cloud in the sky formed over Avignon; perhaps unsurprising, but this was the most innocent-looking cloud of all, and it had little to do with the popes there. It gathered because

Petrarch

of a young man growing up there by the name of Petrarch. Petrarch grew up to be not only a poet, but also the greatest student of classical literature of his day. By the 1330s, Petrarch had come to believe that history consisted of two periods: the glorious classical age of civilization and culture, and what he dubbed 'the Dark Age' of ignorance and barbarism, that had begun with the fall of Imperial Rome in the fifth century and continued up to his own day.

But Petrarch also dreamed of a third and future age (which, presumably, would be brought about by people buying Petrarch's books) in which classical civilization would be reborn.

Excited by the prospect of the rebirth (or 'renaissance') of classical culture, Petrarch's followers, who began to be known as 'humanists', believed that they could end the 'Dark' or 'Middle' Age in their own day. 'Ad fontes!' ('To the sources!') was their battle-cry as they laid siege to the ignorance of their day with the beautiful weapons of classical literature and culture. It was unfortunate for papal Rome, for it was in the darkness of that Middle Age that she had grown, and the light of the new learning would not be kind to her.

A main plank of her power was the 'Donation of Constantine', which purported to be a fourth-century letter from the Roman Emperor Constantine to the pope, explaining that as he moved his capital from Rome to Constantinople (now Istanbul), he was giving the pope lordship over the western half of the Roman Empire. It was on this basis that medieval popes had asserted their political authority over Europe. Popes were superior to kings. However, when a humanist scholar named Lorenzo Valla examined the document, his humanist expertise in Latin enabled him to see that the letter was in fact written using eighth-century, not fourth-century, Latin and terminology. It was a forgery. When he published his findings in 1440, it not only pulled the rug out from under a key papal claim, it cast doubt on all papal claims. For, what other traditional beliefs might be forged?

Valla's greatest legacy, however, was his *Annotations on the New Testament*, a collection of notes never published in his own lifetime. In them, he used his knowledge of Greek to show that there were errors in the official Latin Vulgate translation that the Church used. With the notes unpublished, Valla never lived to see the effect his thoughts would have. However, the greatest humanist scholar of the next generation, Erasmus of Rotterdam, found Valla's *Annotations*, published them, and used them to produce the book that would be used as the greatest weapon against medieval Roman Catholicism.

In 1516, Erasmus went back to the sources and published a Greek edition of the New Testament, putting alongside it, not the official Latin translation, but his own Latin one. In doing so, Erasmus was hoping that a closer attention to the Bible would produce some healthy moral reform in the Church. But he never thought it would do any harm to Rome. He even dedicated it to the pope, who gratefully sent him a letter of thanks and commended it. A little too soon, it would seem. For when Erasmus' New Testament differed from the official Vulgate, it could have

Desiderius Erasmus,
by Hans Holbein the younger

theological implications: in Matthew 4:17, for example, where the Vulgate had Jesus say 'do penance', Erasmus rendered it as 'be penitent', and later 'change your mind'. If Erasmus was right, then Jesus was not instigating the external sacrament of penance, as Rome taught, but speaking of the internal need for sinners to change their minds and turn away from sin. And if Rome was not reading the Bible correctly on that verse, what else might she be getting wrong, and what sort of spiritual authority was she? Erasmus' New Testament was a ticking bomb.

At the same time as their learning was challenging the status quo, humanists, again following Petrarch, tended to be quite critical of the theologians of the day. To the humanists, the theologians only seemed to be interested in the most obscure and irrelevant questions, questions like 'How many angels can dance on the head of a pin?' or 'Could God have become a cucumber instead of a man?' The theologian who characterized such 'subtle' thinking, Duns Scotus, became for the humanists the model of idiocy, and anyone who followed him was lampooned as a 'Duns-man' or 'Dunce', like him.

The theologians were not alone in finding themselves on the business end of humanist satire. The year after Pope Julius II died in 1513, a short sketch called *Julius Excluded from Heaven* started doing the rounds. Erasmus never admitted to writing it (that

would have been a very foolish admission), but the fact that we
have a copy of it in his own handwriting suggests what everyone
suspected. In it, Julius arrives at the gates of heaven, fully clad,
as usual, in his armour, and sporting his trademark beard, which
he had grown as a pledge of vengeance against his many enemies.
Knowing that he might encounter resistance, he had (again, as
usual) brought a sizeable bodyguard who could storm the gates
if necessary. Julius is then made to look rather foolish and vain
by Peter the Gatekeeper, after which the sketch reaches what its
title had made a rather predictable conclusion. In the end, though,
it wasn't so much that humanists could laugh at the expense of
the Church and her theologians, it was what the jokes made clear
that mattered, that with humanism a different approach to truth
had come to challenge the Church's authority: could scholars
know better than the pope? Might Rome and her army of theologians be wrong?

All the controversy stirred
up by the humanists might
not have mattered so much
had their erudition been contained to a few ivory towers.
Technology, however, conspired
with them. Around 1450,
Johannes Gutenberg developed
the first printing press, and
by the 1480s printing shops were
springing up across Europe.
Books could now be produced
in greater numbers and faster
than ever before. Knowledge

could now spread rapidly. It was significant that the first book to
be printed was Gutenberg's Latin Bible: it was time for the age
of the word.

2 God's volcano: Martin Luther

Shortly before midnight on 10 November 1483, in the little mining town of Eisleben in central Germany, a son was born to Hans and Margarete Luder. The next day he was dutifully taken to be baptized, and given the name of that day's saint, Martin. The family came from peasant stock, though the copper mining business was kind to Hans, and he worked hard to improve their state. Over the years it became increasingly clear that young Martin had a bigger brain than most, and Hans was eager to capitalize on it. A career in law would be just the thing for him. He enrolled him at the University of Erfurt, where, in keeping with his father's social aspirations, Martin began to be known by the more polished-sounding name, 'Luther'.

There was only one slight concern for Hans: his son could be rather serious about religion. Martin's hero was Prince Wilhelm of Anhalt, the noble who became a Franciscan monk and was so devoted that he beat and starved himself to death – not the sort of role-model Hans wanted for his promising son. Then the worst happened. Walking back to university after a visit to his parents, the now twenty-one-year-old Martin was suddenly caught in a July storm. A lightning bolt hit so close it knocked him to the ground. Without the chance to make a final confession to a priest, without any last rites, the prospect of what awaited him after death was too terrible to consider. As he hit the ground and the air was forced from him, an involuntary vow came with it: 'Saint Anne, help me! I shall become a monk!' Involuntary it may have been, but a vow was a vow. It was as if a bolt from heaven had forced him to become a monk. His father was furious: wasting all that expensive education; this was no bolt from heaven, it was the devil's work.

Nevertheless, to the monastery Martin went. His hair was shorn so that only a thin circle remained, and he exchanged the clothing of the world for the holy garb of a monk. Being given this new attire was a highly symbolic act, for it was said that a man could restore his innocence by becoming a monk so that he became like a baby freshly washed of its sins in baptism. It was just what Luther wanted: 'We young monks . . . smacked our lips for joy over such delightful talk about our holy monkery.'

Brother Martin at his thinnest. People often commented on his eyes: 'his eyes are piercing and twinkle almost uncannily' said one observer.

To enter the monastery was to enter a world of rules. There were rules for how and when to bow, rules for how to walk, how to talk, where to look and when, rules for how to hold one's eating utensils. Every few hours the monks had to leave their tiny cells and make their way to a service in the chapel, starting with matins in the middle of the night, then another at six in the morning, another at nine, another at twelve, and so on. Otherwise, life was dedicated to climbing the steep ladder to heaven: wearing chafing under-clothes and freezing in the winter cold were thought to be especially pleasing to God, and Luther often took no bread or water for three days at a time (it was only after his Reformation breakthrough that he began to put on weight).

Luther lapped it all up. Yet the more he did, the more troubled he became. All those prayers in chapel, for example: they had to be meant from the heart. Every monk knew he would be judged for all those insincere Our Father's. But had he really meant them enough? And what if he lagged? At some point, every monk found that illness or other duties prevented him from getting to chapel. Some were happy to pay someone else to pray those missed prayers on their behalf. Not Luther: he used his weekends to catch up.

Then there were all the other problems: letting your eyes wander, laughing, poor singing. There were countless sins that needed to be absolved, and Luther was not going to cut corners where his salvation was at stake. Driven to confession, he would exhaust his confessors, taking up to six hours at a time to cata-logue his most recent sins (in the process missing chapel and so adding more prayers to his 'to do' list). Yet Luther was by no means unusual in all this. Monks were urged to ransack their memories for any unconfessed sin. It was expected.

At the end of the confession, one would be absolved by the priest. Unfortunately, though, forgiveness was dependent upon true contrition of heart (as well as performing certain acts of penance). For Luther, who took this seriously, it meant ever-deeper introspection as he analyzed his motivation in confession. Was he truly repentant, or did he just want to avoid being punished by God for what he had done? Such gallows repentance was not acceptable.

His view of things was summed up in 1507, when he was due to say his first mass as a priest. Suddenly, as he stood at the altar, terror overwhelmed him. Now, for the first time in his life, he would have to speak directly to the Judge of all the earth. He had never dared do so before, always praying instead to the saints or Mary. How could he, a sinner, address the Judge?

In all this, he was desperately seeking for a solution to the problem of salvation, a solution that seemed so hidden by all that he knew. Private study of the Bible was not permitted for the monks, but Luther managed to find a quiet spot in the library where he spent his spare time with a Bible, rifling through it for answers, and in the process building up a quite extraordinary knowledge of it.

Then, in 1510, he was given the opportunity of a lifetime: he was sent on monastery business to Rome. For a monk who increasingly knew himself to be spiritually bankrupt, it was like winning the lottery. In Rome, the pilgrim was closer to the apostles and saints than anywhere else. The place was so crammed with their relics (each one conferring various spiritual benefits) that it was a veritable goldmine for the soul. When he caught his first sight of the holy city he prostrated himself on the ground. Then, on arrival, he dashed from holy site to holy site, clocking up merit at each. His one regret during those happy days was that his parents were still alive; had they not been, he could have freed them from purgatory by virtue of all the merit he was amassing. Also, he did not get to say mass in St John Lateran (the performance of which was supposed to achieve instantly the salvation of one's mother).

It was a blissful time in Rome, and yet it was there, in the throbbing heart of Christendom, that the tiniest seeds of doubt were sown in Luther's mind. Rome had become a frenetic spiritual marketplace. With all those people paying for masses to be said for them and their deceased, masses tended to be said at double speed, so fast they could not be understood; in one church two priests even said mass simultaneously at the same altar. It had to get a serious monk thinking. Then he decided to climb the Scala Sancta. This was the staircase which, supposedly, Jesus had climbed to appear before Pilate, and which subsequently had been brought to Rome. By climbing it, kissing each step and repeating the Lord's Prayer for each one, he was assured he could free the soul of his choice from purgatory. Of course, he ran at the chance. Yet on reaching the top he was forced to ask 'Who knows whether it is true?' His doubts were not helped on the way home by his visit to the maid of Augsburg, an old woman who was allegedly nourished by the Mass alone. The fact that she seemed to have no interest in Christian things suggested something odd was going on. Yet in all this, there was no hint that there was a revolution around the corner. The matter was simple: the church just needed a clean-up.

On his return, Luther was transferred to the Augustinian monastery in the tiny mud-cottage town of Wittenberg. His superior had reckoned that with his talent, Luther would make a good teacher of theology (and it would give him the chance to spend time with a Bible, meaning that he might even sort his own spiritual anxieties out). Allowing Luther such freedom with a Bible was a move Rome would soon profoundly regret, but for now, Luther became a teacher of the Bible at the brand new University of Wittenberg.

Wittenberg in 1540

Wittenberg might have been small, but it was the capital of the politically powerful state of Electoral Saxony, and had been blessed by Elector Frederick 'the Wise' by being allowed to host his dazzling collection of relics. It was worth a pilgrimage: the castle church had nine aisles proudly displaying more than 19,000 relics. There you could see a wisp of straw from Christ's crib, a strand of his beard, a nail from the cross, a piece of bread from the Last Supper, a twig from Moses' burning bush, a few of Mary's hairs and some bits of her clothing, as well as

The Holy Roman Empire

Important to Luther's story is the oddity that was the Holy Roman Empire. The Holy Roman Empire was, basically, a rough attempt to get the old Roman Empire back off the ground four hundred years or so after Rome had fallen (only now, being Christian, it was the Holy Roman Empire). The Holy version was a bit smaller than the original though: it basically covered what is now Germany, Austria, Switzerland, the Netherlands, the Czech Republic and bits of northern Italy. In fact, it was hardly an empire at all. By Luther's day, Holy Roman Emperors supervised a hotchpotch of states, many of which were, in reality, ruled by local princes and dukes who simply owed their allegiance to the emperor (and who would meet with him for business at regular imperial councils or 'Diets'). The seven most important of these princes were known as 'Electors', since they would elect new emperors. These Electors were powerful men who could afford to be quite independent-minded. The Electors of Electoral Saxony, where Luther lived, certainly were, and this would prove essential for Luther's survival.

innumerable teeth and bones from celebrated saints. Veneration of each piece was worth an indulgence of 100 days (with a bonus one for each aisle), meaning the pious visitor could tot up more than 1,900,000 days off purgatory.

'When the coin in the coffer rings, the soul from purgatory springs'

So said Johann Tetzel, the travelling televangelist of indulgences, who ignited Luther's fury. Another of his more popular jingles was 'Place your penny on the drum, the pearly gates open and in strolls mum'. With his lurid sermons and his travelling quartet, he was hardly subtle. 'Don't you hear the voices of your wailing dead parents,' he asked his audiences, 'and others, who say, "Have mercy on me, because we are in severe punishment and pain. From this you could redeem us with a small alms".' For that, they were a bargain at the price. He did not even ask people to confess their sins. Just the money would do. And then the indulgence would free you from purgatory, even, he said, if you were guilty of raping the Mother of God. Tetzel was, of course, hugely successful, and while the people got off purgatory, the pope got the money to rebuild St Peter's basilica as the jewel in the crown of the Vatican.

Johann Tetzel

Underneath it all, however, there was a rumble of discontent that German money was being used to finance Italian building projects. But nobody had a problem with it all like Luther. To the devoted monk, the way these indulgences were being offered meant that nobody need really repent of their sins, and that was a scandal. On All Saints' Day (1 November), 1517, the merits of the saints were due to be offered in Wittenberg. And so, on All Saints' Eve, he nailed to the church door a list of ninety-five theses for debate over the matter of indulgences. Everyone would have to see them the next day.

Luther is often imagined angrily and loudly hammering the nails in, his theses a grand protest against Rome, making a spectacular start to the Reformation. However the theses were in Latin, the language of academia, and it was quite usual to post

An indulgence market

notices on the church door. The theses, then, were not a dramatic, popular protest, but a summons to an academic disputation. And, if the ninety-five theses were meant to be a Reformation manifesto, they were a pretty poor effort: they contain not a mention of justification by faith alone, the authority of the Bible, or, indeed, any core Reformation thought. This was because Luther had not yet had his Reformation insight. As such, the theses did not question relics and indulgences as such, only their misuse (it was only much later that he would mockingly describe a greater collection of relics than that in Wittenberg, one that included 'three flames from the burning bush', 'half a wing of the archangel Gabriel' and 'two feathers and an egg from the Holy Spirit'). The theses were an attack on the mistreatment of indulgences from a monk who still worked within the thought-world of medieval Roman Catholicism. The theses affirmed the existence of purgatory, and sought to defend the pope and indulgences from the bad name abuse would give them. In the ninety-five theses, Luther was being a good Catholic.

The ninety-five theses did cause a stir, but it was a stir that might well have blown over had Luther not developed an entirely different understanding of Christianity. Completely unintentionally, Luther had started a chain-reaction: 'God led me into this business against my will and knowledge.'

From son of Rome to heretic

The first reaction came, unsurprisingly, from the indulgence-monger, Johann Tetzel. He immediately issued thunderous demands for Luther to be burned as a heretic, as well as publishing a reply to Luther, in which he argued for the superiority of indulgences over mere acts of love on the basis that self-love is superior to love for neighbour. It did not take long for the clamour against Luther to grow, and the following year, 1518, the pope decided to confer the Golden Rose, the highest honour he could confer, on Elector Frederick the Wise (with the clear understanding that Frederick, in gratitude, would naturally wish to hand Luther over to trial).

Soon, however, a more formidable opponent than Tetzel appeared: Johann Eck. In 1519 Eck skilfully debated Luther in Leipzig, and, in order to secure Luther's condemnation, shrewdly expanded the field of debate by suggesting that the real issue was one of authority. Which had the final say: Bible or pope? It was, of course, a trap, in which, Eck planned, Luther would convict himself. The theologian first appointed by the pope to respond to Luther had already made it clear: even Scripture draws its power and authority from the pope. Would Luther dare to contradict him?

As it happened, Luther walked straight into Eck's ambush, saying that he could understand Scripture without the pope, even against the pope. Eck pounced, calling Luther a disciple of the 'damned and pestiferous' heretics John Wycliffe and Jan Hus. Luther was horrified, denying any such thing. He refused to be an associate of heresy; however, during a break in the debate he looked again at what Hus had taught, and began to see that Eck was right: he was more with Hus than he was with Rome. When he returned and admitted that he did indeed agree with much of what Hus had taught, it was all Eck needed. He immediately made his way to Rome to make sure the pope acted.

More importantly, Eck fertilized Luther's growing doubts about the papacy. Over the following months he became increasingly clear that, if Rome held the pope to be an authority above Scripture, she could never be reformed by God's word. The pope's word would always trump God's. In that case, the reign of the antichrist

'The Birth and Origin of the Pope' by Lucas Cranach the Younger; part of a series of Lutheran propaganda images entitled 'The True Depiction of the Papacy'.

there was sealed, and it was no longer the church of God but the synagogue of Satan.

Entering paradise through open gates

During all this time, Luther's own understanding of Christianity was shifting. It used to be thought that his Reformation insight all came to him in a flash. Older accounts of his life talk about it happening as early as 1513 (hence the idea of the ninety-five theses of 1517 as a proclamation that the Reformation had begun). However, Luther himself was clear that his breakthrough did not come to him until nearly two years *after* the ninety-five theses. It would be the end-point of a long and painful journey.

The reason Luther had posted his ninety-five theses was because he believed the way indulgences were being sold cheapened repentance; and, at the time, repentance was at the heart of Luther's thinking. It had all come about through a deepening sense of the radicality of human sin. Luther had begun to see the extreme naivety of the medieval teaching that 'God will not deny grace to those who do their best'. That suggested that mankind was morally neutral, even good, meaning that our 'best' is acceptable to God. Yet Luther saw the problem is in our hearts: self-love shapes the very grain of our desires. As a result, our 'best' can be nothing more than self-love.

The only answer to this problem of self-love, he reckoned at the time, is self-condemnation. God, in his righteousness, hates and punishes the sin of self-love. If we wish to be saved, we must accept that judgment on us. Instead of calling God a liar by pretending to be righteous and loving, the sinner's task is to say 'Amen' to God's accusation. Only when you admit you are worthy of hell can you be ready for heaven. This was salvation, not by trusting God's promise of salvation, but by accepting his damnation. It was salvation by humility.

This gloomy idea that the only solution for self-love is self-hatred and self-accusation was built upon a frightening view of God. Luther could only see that God was all Judge and no love, his righteousness being all about punishing sinners, his 'gospel' just the promise of judgment. Here was a God he could only ever cower before. Such terror of God

> Luther encountered every time he entered the city church in Wittenberg. On a stone relief above the entrance to the cemetery surrounding the church, Luther saw, carved into the mandorla (an aureole shaped like an almond), Christ seated on the rainbow as judge of the world, so angry the veins stand out, menacing and swollen, on his forehead.[1]

Given Luther's constantly sweeping searchlight-intellect, this was a dark phase of his theology that could never last long. The scheme did not work. Every authority from the Bible to Augustine taught the importance of loving God, but this scheme had no room for loving God. How could one love such a God?

For some time, the answer eluded him. Then, in 1519, when he was looking again at the issues of confession and repentance, it struck him that, after the sinner had confessed, the priest would pronounce God's promise of forgiveness. It was a whole new way of looking at things for Luther: now, the question was, would the sinner trust God's promise? And with that, everything changed. Now he saw that forgiveness is not dependent on how certain the sinner is that he has been truly contrite; forgiveness comes simply by receiving the promise of God. Thus the sinner's hope is found, not in himself, but outside himself, in God's word of promise.

It was while he was thinking these thoughts, studying away in his cell in the monastery tower, that he turned again to that frightening verse about the righteousness of God, Romans 1:17.

> Though I lived as a monk without reproach, I felt that I was a sinner before God with an extremely disturbed conscience. I could not believe that he was placated by my satisfaction. I did not love, yes, I hated the righteous God who punishes sinners, and secretly, if not blasphemously, certainly murmuring greatly, I was angry with God, and said, 'As if, indeed, it is not enough, that miserable sinners, eternally lost through original sin, are crushed by every kind of calamity by the law of the decalogue, without having God add pain to pain by the gospel and also by the gospel threatening us with his righteousness and wrath!' Thus I raged with a fierce and troubled conscience. Nevertheless, I beat importunately upon Paul at that place, most ardently desiring to know what St. Paul wanted.
>
> At last, by the mercy of God, meditating day and night, I gave heed to the context of the words, namely, 'In it the righteousness of God is revealed, as it is written, "He who through faith is righteous shall live."' There I began to understand that the righteousness of God is that by which the

righteous lives by a gift of God, namely by faith. And this is
the meaning: the righteousness of God is revealed by the
gospel, namely, the passive righteousness with which merciful
God justifies us by faith, as it is written, 'He who through faith
is righteous shall live.' Here I felt that I was altogether born
again and had entered paradise itself through open gates.

Here, in this 'tower experience', Luther discovered an entirely
different God and the entirely different way he relates to us. The
righteousness of God, the glory of God, the wisdom of God:
these are not ways in which God is against us. These are things
God has that he shares with us. Here Luther saw for the first time
truly good news of a kind and generous God who gives sinners
the gift of his own righteousness. The Christian life, then, could
not be about the sinner's struggle to achieve his own, paltry
human righteousness; it was about accepting God's own, perfect
divine righteousness. Here now was a God who does not want
our goodness but our trust. All the struggles and all the anxiety
could be replaced with massive confidence and simple faith,
receiving the gift.

It was this good news that reformed Luther's heart, and this
message that he would proclaim to bring reformation to others.
And it soon became clear that this discovery not only gave him
joy and a quite remarkable confidence; it gave him what can
only be seen as a quite superhuman burst of energy to make all
this known.

'The rays of the sun drive out the night'

For the next year, 1520, Luther went into overdrive with writing.
In fact, he was writing faster than three printers could print, and
had to slow down for them. And instead of writing in the Latin
of academia, he wrote in the people's German, so that ordinary
folk, and not just the scholars, could understand his gospel. His

extraordinary speed, his easy style and his explosive message combined with the new-found wonders of the printing press to make Luther, within weeks, the most read German author.

The first main work, *To the Christian Nobility of the German Nation*, was Luther's trumpet blast of reformation against the defensive walls Rome had built around herself. There were three such walls, he said: Rome's first defence was the claim that the pope was the supreme power on earth; the second, that only the pope may interpret the Scriptures; the third, that no one but the pope may summon a council, and thus reform the church. With these walls in place, Rome was impregnable and unreformable. Luther attacked by arguing that there is no distinction between clergy and laity, meaning that the pope's claims were unfounded and that every Christian has the right to interpret Scripture and to call a council to reform the church. How that would change things! Whole new fields of debate opened up once Christians came to believe that they had the right to interpret Scripture themselves, without the pope. It was to provide one of the great challenges of the Reformation: for example, without recourse to a pope, what was to be done when those on the side of the Reformation disagreed over their interpretation of Scripture?

A month later, *The Babylonian Captivity of the Church* appeared. This followed up the first work with an attack on Rome's claim that God's grace flowed only through the sacraments controlled by the priests. If Luther was right that God's gift of righteousness is received with simple trust, that could not be. In fact, he argued, if the Bible and not the pope is to be believed, then there are only

Luther's signature

two sacraments (baptism and the Lord's Supper), not seven, as Rome argued.

The third, and perhaps the most important of Luther's main works that year, was *The Freedom of a Christian*. Having made his attacks, this was his positive explanation of his gospel, and he dedicated it to the pope, since, for all his attacks on Rome and the popes, he wanted to save the man himself. At the heart of it is a story of a king who marries a prostitute, Luther's allegory for the marriage of King Jesus and the wicked sinner. When they marry, the prostitute becomes, by status, a queen. It is not that she made her behaviour queenly and so won the right to the king's hand. She was and is a wicked harlot through and through. However, when the king made his marriage vow, her status changed. Thus she is, simultaneously, a prostitute at heart and a queen by status. In just the same way, Luther saw that the sinner, on accepting Christ's promise in the gospel, is simultaneously a sinner at heart and righteous by status. What has happened is the 'joyful exchange' in which all that she has (her sin) she gives to him, and all that he has (his righteousness, blessedness, life and glory) he gives to her. Thus she can confidently display 'her sins in the face of death and hell and say, "If I have sinned, yet my Christ, in whom I believe, has not sinned, and all his is mine and all mine is his".' This was Luther's understanding of 'justification by faith alone', and it is in that security, he argued, that the harlot actually then starts to become queenly at heart.

Of course, Rome was not going to take all this lying down. Even his positive articulation of the gospel clearly disgusted many.

Luther's new understanding of faith and sin
In *The Freedom of a Christian* Luther showed that, because of his new understanding of the gospel, he was now operating with very different definitions of sin and faith. The things he had understood to be sin (murder,

adultery, etc.) he now understood to be mere symptoms of the real problem: unbelief.

> This is the sin of the world: that it does not believe on Christ. Not that there is no sin against the law besides this; but that this is the real chief sin, which condemns the whole world even if it could be charged with no other sin.

The sinner could therefore be described as 'the man curved in on himself', or 'the man who looks to himself', for sin is not looking to Christ in trust, but looking to oneself. But that is precisely what all his previous efforts at devotion had been: relying on himself!

In contrast, faith was no longer the mere assent of going along to Mass, and nor was it something to 'do'. This is the easy mistake to make when thinking of justification by faith alone: it can sound as if, instead of all the old works and penances, faith is now the one thing we must 'do' – even work hard at – to be saved. The danger then would be that we would fall straight back into Luther's old tortured introspection, wondering if we're 'doing' the act of faith enough. It might be more helpful to describe what Luther discovered as 'justification by God's word' instead of 'justification by faith', because it is God's word that justifies here, not our faith. Faith, thought Luther, is not some inner resource we must summon up; if it was, it would by his definition be sin! For him, the question 'Have I got enough faith?' completely misunderstands what faith is, by looking to and so relying on itself, rather than Christ. Faith is a passive thing, simply accepting, receiving, believing Christ – taking God seriously in what he promises in the gospel.

The inquisitor of Cologne, for example, felt that Luther's allegory of the king and the prostitute made Christ a pimp:

> As if Christ does not take the trouble to distinguish and choose, but simply assumes even the most foul bride and is unconcerned about . . . a pure and honorable lover! As if Christ requires from her only belief and trust and has no interest in her righteousness and other virtues!

There was more than revulsion, though. In 1520, the pope issued a bull (a decree authenticated by the stamp of the pope's own *bulla*, or seal) ordering Luther to recant within sixty days or face excommunication and the ban (under which nobody would be allowed to shelter or sustain him, but were to hand him over). It confirmed Luther in his thinking: nobody had tried to refute him from Scripture, proof to his mind that Rome was not interested in God's word, but only in silencing any threats to her supremacy. Setting herself up above and against God's word, she could only be a tool of Satan. His blistering response was a tract entitled *Against the Execrable Bull of Antichrist*.

The papal bull excommunicating Luther

Then, when the sixty days' reprieve was up, the people of Wittenberg were invited to the carrion pit outside one of the city gates. Luther appeared and threw his copy of the bull into the fire with the words, 'Because you have confounded the truth of God, today the Lord confounds you. Into the fire with you!' With it went a number of works of theology and books of canon law, symbolically destroying the entire ecclesiastical system of the Roman church.

Then, nothing happened. Technically, Luther was now excommunicated and under the ban, but already the authority of Rome was being flouted. It was a situation the Holy Roman Emperor could not tolerate. Luther was summoned to appear before him at the next imperial council at Worms. From that moment, Luther faced the wrath of the emperor, the pope, burning at the stake and the prospect of hell ever after if he was wrong. It is testimony to the transformatory power of his gospel-discovery that the once frightened monk in the thunderstorm would now stare them all down with the immovable affirmation 'Here I stand!'

Kidnapped

After his hearing, it had not taken long for the emperor to declare Luther to be 'an obstinate schismatic and manifest heretic' who should be harboured by none and read by none, on pain of the direst punishment. Luther, however, was not waiting around

A nineteenth-century illustration of Luther before the Diet of Worms

in Worms to be condemned. He had already boarded a wagon for Wittenberg.

Yet, en route, as the wagon entered a narrow, wooded gorge, a group of horsemen surrounded Luther's party, aiming their crossbows. Amid curses, Luther was snatched and galloped away. Everyone knew what had happened: Luther had been seized for a quiet and summary execution. 'O God,' wrote the artist Albrecht Dürer, 'if Luther is dead, who now will teach us the holy Gospel so clearly?' It was just what they were meant to think. The kidnappers were, in fact, in the employ of Elector Frederick the Wise, who had devised the plan to keep Luther in safe custody without incurring the dangers of being seen to harbour an outlaw. And they had not taken him to a hidden grave, but, after zig-zagging through the area to throw off any pursuers, they had arrived, late that night, at the Wartburg castle, Frederick's stronghold in Electoral Saxony.

It was to be Luther's secret home for the next ten months – and the setting for some of his most extraordinary achievements. He grew a beard and let his hair grow to cover his monk's haircut, and was soon unrecognizable in a set of knight's clothes. Martin Luther the outlaw had disappeared; this character was known as 'Sir George'. It seemed appropriate for a dragon-slayer. For all the excitement and triumph he could have felt, he found his time in the castle extremely difficult. He was lonely and sick. Yet he worked with a frenzy that outdid even the previous year's efforts. Unable to preach to a congregation, he wrote a book of model sermons. And, among other things, in less than eleven weeks, he managed to translate Erasmus' Greek New Testament into German. It took a bit of polishing up before it was ready (and a few illustrations were added, a panorama of Rome next to Revelation's description of the destruction of Babylon, for example), but amazingly, in that time Luther had produced a masterpiece. The language was so punchy, so colourful, so of the street, that it transformed the very way people spoke German. Luther was becoming the father of the modern German language.

More importantly, with its publication in September 1522, Luther realized his dream that the people 'might seize and taste the clear, pure Word of God itself and hold to it'.

By letters he also sought to encourage the Reformation back in Wittenberg. A characteristic bit of pastoral advice would involve shocking the reader into a clearer appreciation of the gospel. 'Be a sinner and sin boldly,' he wrote to one young friend who was tempted to make his own piety the ground of his confidence before God,

> but believe and rejoice in Christ even more boldly, for he is victorious over sin, death, and the world. As long as we are here [in this world] we have to sin. This life is not the dwelling place of righteousness, but, as Peter says, we look for new heavens and a new earth in which righteousness dwells. It is enough that by the riches of God's glory we have come to know the Lamb that takes away the sin of the world. No sin will separate us from the Lamb, even though we commit fornication and murder a thousand times a day. Do you think that the purchase price that was paid for the redemption of our sins by so great a Lamb is too small?

Also at the Wartburg, Luther suffered from temptations and assaults which would never really leave him. 'My temptation is this, that I think I don't have a gracious God.' That might seem an odd temptation after everything he had been through, but he saw it as the devil's assault on him, and it forced him to be an expert physician of doubt. Not that that was always obvious. Sometimes he would roar scornful abuse at the tempter: 'But if that is not enough for you, Devil, I have also shit and pissed; wipe your mouth on that and take a hearty bite.' Other times he would defecate on him, or throw his inkpot at him, leaving, for the Luther pilgrims to admire, an ink-stain (regularly touched up, of course, so as to heighten the sense of devotion – relics came back so easily).

Many find this side of Luther rather troubling. Was he unhinged? Clearly, Luther was no clean and starchy Christian hero; he was very earthy. Yet it would be wrong to write off these battles with the devil as the fits of a dirty-minded lunatic. His assaults do not fit medical diagnoses or patterns of normal depression. And his responses had a point: Luther held satanically-inspired doubt as something to be excreted, rejected, risen above and derided with laughter. It was too subtle and tempting to be engaged head-on.

At other times, he battled his doubts by writing a relevant Bible verse on his wall, on a piece of furniture, or, indeed, on anything to hand. Again, it is highly revealing. He knew that within himself there was only sin and doubt. All his hope lay outside himself, in God's word. There his security before God was unaffected by how he felt or how he did. And so, when facing doubt, he would not look within himself for any comfort (that would be faithlessness and sin, the origin of all anxiety, not the cure!); instead, he would hold before his eyes this unchanging, external word.

How to reform a church

Meanwhile, back in Wittenberg, those in charge were making it look as if the Reformation was really all about attacking priests and the images of saints, eating as much as possible on fast days, and generally doing everything differently just so as to cock a snook at the old ways. To Luther's mind, it was a mad mistake. It was just as bad as Rome in getting obsessed with the externals, and then enforcing certain behaviour. The problem he saw in the church was not physical images; first, the images needed to be removed from hearts.

Luther came out of hiding, returned to Wittenberg, and, instead of using force to reform, sought to persuade people with the Scriptures through simple, clear preaching. He believed that the word of God must first convince people, and then the rotten old structures would collapse. It was exactly what he had stood for before the emperor, that it is the Scriptures that must drive and dictate thought and practice. As a result, Luther never believed that he should devise any great programme for spreading the Reformation. He simply wanted to unleash the word of God, and let that do all the work.

Still, doing just that was a simply enormous task. As things stood, the very structure of every church service militated against the Bible being opened. So Luther re-wrote the liturgy to make it a Bible teacher. Among other changes was the introduction of congregational singing (before, the people did little more than watch the priests). To ensure the content of what was being sung, Luther composed hymns for them (he was a man for whom the ear mattered, loving both words and music). Probably the best known was that battle-hymn of the Reformation, 'A Mighty Fortress is our God', the words of which made Luther's ideas familiar to millions:

> The Prince of Darkness grim, we tremble not for him;
> His rage we can endure, for lo, his doom is sure,
> One little word shall fell him.

On top of all this, he restructured the way the church was run; provided preachers for other towns; encouraged and advised kings and princes interested in the Reformation, from Sweden to Transylvania; and wrote catechisms (basic explanations of the faith designed to be memorized). The catechism was something Luther took very seriously. He believed that everyone should memorize it, that anyone unwilling to learn it should be barred from the Lord's Supper, that parents should withhold food and drink from such children, and that, ultimately, such people should be exiled. He knew he could not force belief, but he insisted that the people at least know the truth. And, in many ways, it seemed to work. Within a few years, he reckoned that fifteen-year-olds in Wittenberg knew more about the word of God 'than all the universities and doctors before'.

Katie

It was not long before most of the monks had left Luther's monastery in Wittenberg. And for those who stayed, life no longer revolved around the countless services; now their spare time was spent talking about the new theology over mugs of beer. Soon Luther was the only one left, and after that, the Elector decided to give the whole monastery to Luther to be his own, substantial, home.

In fact, everywhere monasteries and nunneries seemed to be emptying as monks and nuns heard of Luther's discovery and abandoned Catholicism. In 1523, one group of nuns in a different German state (where the ruler executed runaway nuns) wrote to ask Luther what they should do. He advised escape, and even arranged it. Enjoying the symbolism, he sent a herring merchant to their convent on Easter morning, his covered wagon full of herring barrels. Nine nuns hopped in and were smuggled all the way to a new life in Wittenberg.

Ex-nuns, of course, had no social security whatsoever, and so Luther felt it his duty to find them all husbands. He managed for eight of them, but the ninth, Katharina von Bora, was a struggle. For a while, the last thing on Luther's mind was marriage for himself. He assumed it would not be long before he was burned as a heretic, on top of which he had to face repeated attempts on his life, and therefore, he felt, it would not be fair for him to take a wife. However, for all his immovability before pope and emperor, over the next two years the badgering of his friends and the feisty ninth nun wore him down. He married Katharina, fifteen years his junior, in 1525.

It is clear that Martin and Katie enjoyed each other's company, whether walking in the garden, fishing together or eating with friends. Their letters to each other, written when Luther was travelling, are full of jokes and clear affection. And she was spirited enough to stand up to the indomitable Reformer. 'In domestic affairs I defer to Katie. Otherwise I am led by the Holy Spirit.' As such, Luther would have to resort to bribes to get her to read her Bible more.

The household they built together in the old cloister was a rollicking, rambunctious affair, filled over the years with three sons, two daughters, a pet dog and innumerable visitors, relatives and students. Luther had a bowling alley built in the garden for when he broke from his study or prayer (he would pray for at least three hours a day, working through Bible verses and bluntly holding out God's promises, demanding that he keep them). Katie ran their sizable private brewery, selling some of the beer to help make ends meet, and using the rest to lubricate all those theological discussions over mealtimes and into the evenings. That didn't stop her from occasionally upbraiding Martin for drinking too freely at such occasions, nor from feelings of annoyance when students spent mealtimes taking notes instead of eating. Twice, however, tragedy struck: both daughters died young, one of them, Magdelene, in Martin's arms. He was overcome with tears, and yet did his best to console the rest of the family with the hope of the gospel. 'She will rise again at the last day' he declared over the coffin. It was said with a confidence he once would have considered a presumptuous sin.

What is this Reformation?

Around the same time that Martin was getting together with Katie, he was engaged in what was, perhaps, the most significant dialogue of the Reformation. It was with the scholar who had published the Greek New Testament that had converted him: Erasmus. Here were two ex-Augustinian monks, out to reform the church. Yet, as their dialogue showed, they had very different ideas of what that reform should look like. For Erasmus, it was simple: he wanted nothing more than to give the church a good, moral bath. Scrub away the corruption, wash off the hypocrisy, and all would be well. Over the years, however, he became increasingly troubled by the fact that Luther meant something entirely different by 'reformation'. Where he wanted to call popes to be better popes, Luther wanted to get rid of popes altogether. Where he wanted to clean up the Roman Catholic system, Luther wanted to burn it all down and replace it.

And so, in 1524, Erasmus wrote *On the Freedom of the Will*, in which he argued that, while of course Luther was right to say that we can never really earn merit before God, he had gone too far. For, Erasmus purred, God is like a loving father, and takes our fumbling efforts and smiles on them as if they really were worth something. Erasmus always liked to position himself as the wise man, above the crude extremes of more petty minds, and this was typical Erasmus, aiming at a sophisticated middle position between Rome and the Reformation. But of course, he smiled, like Luther he wanted to uphold God's grace. Yet surely God would reward a good deed? Quite simply, he could not understand that Luther placed all his certainty of salvation on Christ alone, and not on his own performance at all.

The differences all came from how Luther and Erasmus understood Christianity. Erasmus was the sort who was always saying how things in the Bible were so much more complicated than they appear at first sight. Thus the masses would either need a great mind like his to understand them, or, if even he could not understand them (and this applied to many things) then they must be numbered among the countless mysteries of that obscure text, the Bible. Given how unclear the Bible was, he deemed that Christians should not try to settle doctrinal questions such as the Trinity, God's role in salvation, and other such tricky issues. God had left them vague, and therefore they must be unimportant, and probably unhelpfully distracting from the more important business of getting on with Christian living. 'The sum of our religion is peace and unanimity,' he once said, 'but these can scarcely stand unless we define as little as possible'.

> Christianity, to Erasmus, was essentially morality, with a minimum of doctrinal statement loosely appended . . . Luther's attitude was very different. To him, Christianity was a matter of doctrine first and foremost, because true religion was first and foremost a matter of faith; and faith is correlative to truth . . . Christianity was to Luther a dogmatic religion, or it was nothing . . . Erasmus' conception of an undogmatic Christianity, and the humanist's airy indifference to matters of doctrine seemed to him as essentially un-Christian as anything well could be.[2]

Erasmus was, at the time, the most revered scholar in the world, and since *On the Freedom of the Will* came from so eminent a figure (and one who had been so instrumental in his own conversion), Luther actually read it. Usually he only read a couple of pages of polemics against himself before using them as toilet paper. Because of Erasmus' scholarly reputation, it looked like he was the heavyweight; but this was theology, and Erasmus was no theologian. In this arena, Erasmus was like an ant attacking a rhino.

Luther responded with *The Bondage of the Will*, savaging Erasmus' half-baked arguments. And it really was a savaging. Luther refused to talk about the heart of how to be saved in Erasmus' cool, dispassionate style. He thought Erasmus had been worryingly glib about the key issue: are we able to do anything toward our salvation? In complete contrast to Erasmus, Luther was adamant that, for all we freely choose to do, we never naturally choose to please God, and therefore all our salvation must be God's doing, not ours.

> The difference is evidenced in the words used by the two men to describe their depressions. Luther called his *Anfechtung*. The word suggests an assault from without, an attack by the Devil. The

only hope lay in a conquest from without by Christ, who for us overcame the Devil, Death, and Hell. Erasmus called his depressions *pusillanimitas*, literally, weakness of spirit, faint-heartedness, for which we have the little-used English derivative, pusillanimity. This implies a weakness within, which man can do something to remedy by pulling himself together. In Luther's case moral effort was useless, but not so for Erasmus.[3]

Because Erasmus failed to rely entirely upon God's grace, Luther concluded sadly that Erasmus must be a stranger to it. With his Greek New Testament, he had, like Moses, led many out of slavery; yet like Moses he never entered the Promised Land. The stark difference between them showed that reform of abuses and the Reformation were two completely distinct projects. The former was a call for man to do better; the latter was an admission that he cannot, and hence must rely on the all-sufficient grace of God that the moralizers implicitly denied.

Handing on the Reformation

In 1530, nine years after Luther had appeared before him at Worms, Emperor Charles V decided to hold another imperial diet, this time at Augsburg. The forces of Islam had got as far as Vienna, and were an imminent threat to Christendom (they would remain so until a hundred and fifty years later, when the crescent of Islam was defeated outside Vienna, and the Viennese ate croissants in celebration). Charles wanted to face them with a united Christian force, which meant he needed to deal with the religious differences in the empire.

Of course, Luther couldn't go himself. He was still a condemned heretic under the emperor's ban. Nevertheless, in Augsburg, his young colleague, Philipp Melanchthon, composed a Lutheran confession of faith for submission to the emperor. Luther was delighted with it. The emperor was not. However, nine princes of the empire signed the confession; and with that, Lutheranism became, officially, a serious force to be reckoned with. Things had changed since the last diet and that showdown between emperor and monk.

Behind much of this early growth of the Reformation was Luther's never-tiring pen. It poured forth volumes of Bible commentaries, books of sermons, tracts and works of theology. More important than them all, though, in 1534 he completed his translation of the Old Testament into German, and published it with prefaces, marginal notes and illustrations. 'Here you will find the swaddling cloths and the manger in which Christ lies', announced the preface. Luther always emphasized that all the Scriptures are only ever about Christ, for it is only through faith in him that any could ever be saved. He took against the book of James for exactly this reason; he felt it was not full enough of Christ. One Sunday, when the set Bible passage for the day was from James, he just read the text, and then told the congregation 'I don't want to preach on this', and went on to preach on something else.

Der Prophet Hesekiel.

Woodcut of Ezekiel 1 by
Lucas Cranach the Younger,
Wittenberg Bible 1541

The death that he had once so feared crept up slowly on Luther. What had changed was that now he longed to see Christ. However, it was a painful decline. The constant and immense demands on him ravaged his health. In 1534 he suffered the first of a number of heart attacks. When on the move, he suffered

Luther and the Jews

What probably turns more people away from Luther
than anything else is his tract *On the Jews and Their Lies*.
Trumpeted and used as traditional German virtue by the
Nazis in the twentieth century, and displayed in a glass
case at the Nuremberg rallies, it is enough for many to
dismiss Luther as an odious anti-Semite, and all his
theology as fatally tainted. Undoubtedly it contains
horrible material that one wishes he had died before
writing. However, not only was it written long after his
Reformation breakthrough, after a change of heart
toward the Jews (meaning that it is entirely inappropriate
to tar all his theology with its brush), but also, the
caricature is a distortion. There was no racism involved.

In 1523 he wrote *That Jesus Christ was Born a Jew*, a
critique of the common mistreatment of Jews by
Christians. He dedicated it to a converted Jew he had
befriended, whom he would later support financially (and
whose son he would house) at great personal cost. Over
the years, though, he detected what he saw as a hardness
of heart in the unbelieving Jews, in that they refused to
acknowledge that their own Scriptures pointed them
clearly to Christ. Finally stung into action by some
virulent Jewish apologetics that attacked Christianity, in
1542 he wrote *On the Jews and Their Lies*. In it he argued,
first, that being children of Abraham was always a
spiritual matter, not one of genetics; he then went on to
show from the Old Testament that Jesus must be the
promised Christ; only then did he move on to his
notorious set of recommendations. While he condemned
personal acts of vengeance, he argued that then-standard
blasphemy laws should be applied to the Jews, making
their religion criminal. As such, Jewish synagogues and
houses should be destroyed as dangerous hotbeds of

blasphemy; and, along with other blasphemers, the Jews themselves should be expelled.

It is hard for a modern audience, not only to avoid reading later racial anti-Semitism into such unpleasant material, but also to understand that these were, at the time, standard measures taken against heretics. Luther was arguing for the powers of the state to be applied to uphold Christianity. And, while his recommendations are repulsive, they had not come from a lack of spiritual concern. Concluding the work, he wrote: 'May Christ, our dear Lord, convert them mercifully and preserve us steadfastly and immovably in the knowledge of him, which is eternal life. Amen.'

from a painful abscess on his leg as well as often excruciating kidney stones; when working, he battled with severe headaches, dizzy spells and a loud ringing and roaring in his ears.

Yet to the end he had a personality that could set the Rhine on fire. Some loved it, others wished he could be at least a little less rude and raw. Certainly he was no stained-glass ideal. Perhaps, though, such a red-blooded and blunt man was just what was needed for the momentous and seemingly impossible task of challenging all Christendom and turning it around. He was shock-therapy for the world. And, somehow, his personality seems fit for the gospel he uncovered: he inspires no moral self-improvement in would-be disciples; instead, his evident humanity testifies to a sinner's absolute need for God's grace.

In January 1546, Luther was sixty-three, and considered himself very old. Against Katie's fears, he braved the freezing Saxon winter to journey to Eisleben, the town where he was born, to settle a dispute. Once there, sensing that he did not have long, his thoughts turned to his own resurrection after death; over supper the conversation was about whether or not we will recognize each other in the resurrection. He was certain we would.

After the meal, he felt pains and a tightening in his chest. Taking to bed, he prayed Psalm 31:5 ('Into your hands I commit my spirit') and then jokingly ordered those with him to pray 'for our Lord God and his gospel, that all might be well with him, for the Council of Trent and the accursed pope are very angry with him'. The joke had a serious point: his own death did not matter, for the gospel is God's power for salvation and cannot be silenced by the death of a servant or the raging of an enemy. Finally, in what almost looks like an ultimate repeat of his trial at Worms, he was asked 'are you ready to die trusting in your Lord Jesus Christ and to confess the doctrine which you have taught in his name?' A clear 'Yes' was his answer. Soon after, he took his last breath. There was no priest present, there were no sacraments administered, and no last confession was made. Instead there was simple confidence before God. It was all testimony to how his teaching had changed things.

Luther was buried, appropriately, beneath his own pulpit. Years before, when Luther was kidnapped and feared dead, Albrecht Dürer had cried, 'O God, if Luther is dead, who now will teach us the holy Gospel so clearly?' Now that he really was dead, the question was: could they really believe Luther, that all would be well with the Lord God and his gospel?

Notes

1 Oswald Bayer, 'Justification: Basis and Boundary of Theology', in Joseph A. Burgess and Marc Kolden (eds.), *By Faith Alone: Essays in Honor of Gerhard O. Forde* (Eerdmans, 2004), p. 78.

2 J. I. Packer, and O. R. Johnston, 'Historical and Theological Introduction' to *Martin Luther on The Bondage of the Will* (James Clarke & Co., 1957), pp. 43–44.

3 R. Bainton, *Erasmus of Christendom* (William Collins Sons & Co., 1969), p. 33.

3 Soldiers, sausages and revolution: Ulrich Zwingli and the Radical Reformers

Martin Luther was not alone as a prophet of reformation. Within two months of Luther's birth, 'God's mercenary', Ulrich (or Huldrych) Zwingli, was born in the pretty Swiss alpine village of Wildhaus.

The Alps are lovely – Zwingli always thought so – but it was not easy to scratch a living off them in the fifteenth century, and many Swiss found that easier money could be had through becoming a hired mercenary. And they were clearly good at it: the brave and disciplined Swiss pikemen and William Tell-like crossbow-marksmen were feared across Europe for their military prowess. Glory days were soon to follow with Julius II, a pope who spent more time in armour at the head of papal armies than he did saying Mass in Rome. He wanted Swiss muscle to make up his personal bodyguard, and to provide the backbone of his army.

None of this might have seemed very relevant to Ulrich Zwingli when, aged 22, he became the parish priest of the little town of Glarus. He was set on a comfortable career path in the church. Yet Glarus was virtually a military camp, providing some of the biggest contingents of men for the papal army. A fierce patriot anyway, Zwingli decided to join his men as an army chaplain, and go to fight for the Holy Father and Mother Church. The experience would change him forever. In 1515, they met the gigantic army of King Francis I of France at Marignano, outside Milan. It was a slaughter in which over 10,000 Swiss died. Zwingli's romantic view of the noble Swiss fighting with honour for a holy cause was drowned in their blood. He realized he had misunderstood both warfare and the pope. The shock forced him to wonder what else he might have misunderstood.

A strange new world

Once back home in Glarus, he realized that he had spent years reading Bible commentaries, but that he had not read the Bible

HVLDRYCHVS ZVINGLIVS

Ulrich Zwingli

itself. So in 1516 he bought a copy of Erasmus' Greek New Testament, hot off the press, and took the revolutionary step of trying to understand it. It hardly sounds revolutionary today, but that only shows how profoundly the Reformation changed Europe. At the time, to go straight to the Bible and seek to understand it was considered dangerously subversive. Without the pope's guidance, people could make the Bible say anything. Worse, it implied that the pope was not God's appointed interpreter of Scripture. It was a slippery slope to schism, to walking away from the embrace of Mother Church. Zwingli experienced more than the thrill of rule-breaking, though. As he opened his New Testament he enjoyed what hardly anyone in Europe had enjoyed for a millennium: he could read the very word of God, the real thing, the very words the Holy Spirit had given to the apostles to write. He was so excited he copied out most of Paul's letters and memorized almost the entire New Testament in Greek.

It was for Zwingli a journey like that of Columbus twenty years earlier: he found a new world in the Bible, a world he had never dreamed of. Yet if this was when Zwingli was converted, it was not a conversion Luther-style. He had no real problem with the cult of saints, becoming priest of the shrine of the 'black Virgin' of Einsiedeln in 1516; and he had no real problem with the papacy, happily receiving a papal pension for his services in the papal army. In fact, two years later, a month after Luther had been summoned to Rome for questioning, he was appointed a papal chaplain. He would remain part of the Roman system for a few years yet, but all the time his theology was evolving. His papal pension he spent on books, and he began studying Hebrew so that he might also read the Old Testament just as, he saw, God had dictated it.

Meanwhile the flocks of pilgrims who came to Einsiedeln spread his reputation as a preacher. And thus it was that, in 1518, the village boy with the thick yokel accent was appointed as a preacher in the Great Minster in Zurich. It was not a popular appointment; though people had no problem with his views, he was opposed because he admitted that he had recently visited a prostitute. However, he seemed genuinely repentant, and in any case, that little kafuffle was almost immediately eclipsed by what Zwingli did next. On Saturday 1 January, 1519 (his thirty-fifth birthday) he stepped into the pulpit under the high steeples of the Great Minster, and announced that, rather than preach through set readings and fill his sermons with the thoughts of medieval theologians, he would preach his way through Matthew's Gospel verse by verse. And when he had finished that, he'd keep going through the rest of the New Testament. God's word would go out to all the people, undiluted, unadulterated, constantly: this was what Zwingli would be all about, and this was how Zurich would be reformed.

There was just one more event that was to change Zwingli

significantly. In 1519 the plague hit Zurich and nearly carried Zwingli off with it. It was just as epochal for him as when Luther was almost hit by lightning fourteen years earlier: brought to the edge of death's abyss he was forced to look into eternity. Only, where Luther had prayed to St Anne, Zwingli found he could only rely exclusively upon God's mercy. When he recovered, he was a changed man, a man on a mission to do something bold for God. Now he clearly saw all trusting in created things, whether saints or sacraments, to be gross idolatry. He was going to lead peoples' hearts from idols to the living God of mercy.

'The Dance of Death'
by Hans Holbein

The gentle soldier

This still did not mean burning papal bulls and writing tracts against Rome, though. While Luther was doing all that, Zwingli was joining the Roman Catholic hierarchy by accepting the position of canon in the Great Minster. Zwingli was extremely cautious by temperament, allowing him at times to be cowardly, and this meant that the Reformation in Zurich was less explosively dramatic than it often was elsewhere. This was coupled with the fact that Rome relied on Swiss mercenaries and so, while increasingly disturbed by reports from Zurich, popes did not feel they could afford to annoy the town by excommunicating Zwingli. As late as 1523, before realizing that no more men were coming from Zurich to fight for Rome, the pope felt he could write a friendly and flattering letter to Zwingli.

In consequence, some radicals in Zurich began to see Zwingli as a bottleneck, restricting the flow of the Spirit being poured out for the work of reformation. They wanted to remove the hindrance and force the pace. However, lack of drama in Zurich should not be confused too easily with lack of reformation. Zwingli knew that getting the hammers out, however exciting, would not effect real change. Rather, he believed, the true secret of reform is to change individual hearts by the application of the gospel. External reformation of the churches must flow from that inward conversion if it is to be anything more than cosmetic surgery. Thus, instead of campaigning for change, Zwingli dedicated himself to preaching God's word. Having primed the people, he would then wait for them to demand the change God's word requires. The results were not speedy, but they had an almost unique durability even beyond his own death. When changes came in Zurich, they came from deep and popular conviction that God's word commanded them, and so they stuck.

The Clarity and Certainty of the Word of God
In 1522 Zwingli wrote this, one of his greatest works, on the power and effectiveness of God's word. In it, he starts by looking at Genesis 1:26, where he sees the three Persons of the Trinity working together to create humanity in their likeness. Because this happened, Zwingli says, humanity, being made in the image of this God, always secretly longs for the word of God. We aren't aware that this is what we long for, but this is the desire behind all our longings: we crave the life and light that the word of God brings.

It is these two characteristics of God's word that Zwingli really wants to look at: that it is a word of life-giving power and a word of enlightenment. First, he says, the word of God has certainty (when God speaks, it happens, as for instance when he said 'Let there be light!'). Second, the word of God has clarity. By this he meant that, not only is it intelligible, but more, that it actually brings its own enlightenment. We do not have to be previously enlightened to understand God's word, for we do not bring our own light to the word. On the contrary, the word is light and brings light to our natural darkness. This belief was essential to Zwingli's reformation project: he could preach the Scriptures to all because the Scriptures can be understood by all. They were no longer to be the preserve of the educated elite. But by saying that God's word brings its own enlightenment, Zwingli also meant that we do not recognize the Bible to be God's word because of what anyone tells us or because of any rational argument, but because when God speaks, we are compelled to recognize his word for what it is. We know the Scriptures are divine, not when the pope says so, but when we read them. If we fail to see that, the fault lies with us, he says:

> Consider a good strong wine. To the healthy it tastes excellent. It makes him merry and strengthens him and warms his blood. But if there is someone who is sick of a disease or fever, he cannot even taste it, let alone drink it, and he marvels that the healthy is able to do so. This is not due to any defect in the wine, but to that of the sickness. So too it is with the Word of God. It is right in itself and its proclamation is always for good. If there are those who cannot bear or understand or receive it, it is because they are sick.

It is this high view of Scripture that was the motor for the transformation of Zurich. God's word, he said, is like a mighty, unstoppable river. It can be preached with the utmost confidence, for it is God's effective power to create, save and change the world.

Changes came, and not everyone liked it: genuine Catholics who objected to Zwingli's theology; monks who feared being turfed out of their monasteries; those who simply disliked change. Soon, dark rumours about Zwingli began to be heard on the streets: he was a spy in the service of the King of France or (extraordinarily) of the pope; he was a profligate (opening that old sore); he was a heretic; maybe he was even the antichrist.

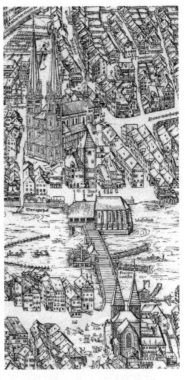

The Great Minster in Zurich

Malicious gossip was one thing, but being called a heretic called into question the very essence of the Reformation. Zwingli leapt to defend his theology, and, five years after Martin Luther wrote his ninety-five theses, Zwingli wrote sixty-seven. But, where Luther had confined himself to an attack on indulgences and corrupt medieval theology, Zwingli laid out a much more comprehensive outline of Reformation thought. In them he argued that Christ, the true head of the Church, rules his church through his word, not through the pope. Thus the Bible, not the pope, is master. This was a stab straight to the heart of the pope's claims and power. He also argued that Christ's death on the cross was a complete sacrifice and so does not need to be repeated constantly in the Mass. This was to challenge the very purpose of the priesthood, for celebrating Mass was what they did. He savaged the practice of praying to saints, denied the existence of purgatory, and argued that only trust in Christ, not our own good works, can save. It was the first volley Zwingli had fired directly at Rome. But it was a heavy one.

Did Zwingli steal from Luther?
Zwingli always claimed that he had come to his views without Luther's help:

> The papists say, 'You must be Lutheran, because you preach just as Luther writes.' I reply, 'I preach just as Paul writes. Why not call me a Pauline?' . . . I will not be called by Luther's name, for I have read little of his teaching. I will have no name except that of my captain, Christ, whose soldier I am. Yet I value Luther as highly as anyone alive.

Many think the idea that Zwingli could have come to such 'Lutheran' views independently but almost simultaneously is just too great a coincidence to be believed. So was he in fact a closet follower of Luther who just pretended to have made his own discovery in order to get the glory?

Probably not. The whole tone of Zwingli's thought is quite different from Luther's, and he puts emphasis on different things. For example, while with Luther Zwingli most definitely believed in justification by faith alone, it never had the same prominence in his thinking as it did

---

for Luther. And it didn't mean quite the same thing. Luther believed that when Adam sinned and was declared guilty, the entire human race became, as it were, 'clothed' in his guilt; but when we turn to Christ we are 'clothed' in his righteousness. Zwingli, on the other hand, believed more that we each become guilty when we actually sin, but that Christ makes us righteous in ourselves. Luther's idea that believers are at the same time righteous (in status before God) and sinful (in heart), did not really figure in Zwingli's mind. Instead, Zwingli's emphasis was more on idolatry, the problem of trusting in creatures rather than the Creator.

If there was an influence on Zwingli other than the Bible, it was probably Erasmus more than Luther. Like Erasmus, but very unlike Luther, he would quote Plato as happily as Paul to make his points. Like Erasmus, he tended to think of Christ as an example for us, more than as our saviour. This definitely must not be overplayed: again and again one reads in Zwingli lines such as 'For just as Abraham embraced Jesus his blessed seed, and through him was saved, so also today we are saved through him.' Yet still, salvation gets less attention from Zwingli. The result was that their messages looked quite different: where Luther opened the Bible to find Christ, Zwingli sought more simply to open the Bible.

The differences between them grew into tensions over the years, until in 1529 the two men finally met. Philip, the Protestant ruler of Hesse in central Germany, invited them both to his castle in Marburg in an attempt to unite Protestantism. They found they agreed on most things, but on the Lord's Supper they were irreconcilable. Luther believed that Christ's body and blood are really present in the bread and wine, making the Lord's Supper a gift of grace from God. Those who receive Christ in faith are blessed, those who take the Supper without faith face special judgment for despising Christ when offered to them. Zwingli maintained that Christ's body cannot literally be present in the bread, but is instead symbolized by the bread. The Lord's Supper for him was a mere symbol to help us commemorate Christ's sacrifice and to signify our membership of his body. Luther was horrified. It looked to him as though Zwingli was turning the Supper into an opportunity for us to do something (i.e. commemorate and signify something about us). This, surely, meant that the Lord's Supper would no longer be about grace but works. Believing that Zwingli had fatally compromised the gospel, Luther refused to partner with him. The reformations in Wittenberg and Zurich would, henceforth, go it alone.

Zurich recruited

It was time for a showdown between Zwingli and his opponents. A public debate was arranged for 29 January 1523, and there Zwingli was to defend his views. When the day came, the City Hall was packed out, for this was to be a tense theological prize fight, with the future of Zurich at stake. Zwingli walked in, and almost immediately it was clear that he was the better armed. He spoke with large copies of the Greek New Testament, the Hebrew Old Testament and the Latin Vulgate open in front of him. And it was clear he knew them well; he was able to cite long passages in the original from memory. In short, he was unbeatable, and the debate a complete triumph for him. Nobody dared face up to such a theological heavyweight with the charge of heresy. Better, Zwingli so carried the day that the city council immediately ruled that only preaching that was biblical would be legal in Zurich.

Of course, that changed everything. But the first question now was: how could it happen? Very few knew their Bibles well enough to be able to preach really biblically. And so Zwingli set about the creation of a school for preachers. The first stage was a grammar school for boys, to get them literate. After that, the next stage was a theological college. There the students were, as Zwingli put it, 'given the gift of tongues' (the knowledge of Hebrew, Greek and Latin) and taught how to 'prophesy' (preach). With their days spent in Bible study and lectures in theology, a whole generation of pastors and missionaries arose who were well trained in the knowledge of the Bible. Out of the study times came commentaries on many books of the Bible, as well as a complete translation which was then richly illustrated and published as the Zurich Bible in 1531. Thus Zwingli loaded

---

Anna Zwingli

Quite early on, Zwingli became convinced that Rome was wrong to insist on the celibacy of its priests. The Bible taught no such thing. Yet he believed that if he actually got married it would be an unnecessary stumbling-block to those who had not yet come round to his view of the Bible's authority over the pope. Thus, in 1522, he secretly married Anna Reinhart. Only after two years did he feel the people would be able to accept this, and then they officially married, going on to have several children, most of whom died in infancy.

At home, Zwingli showed that, while he disapproved of music in church, he was in fact an accomplished musician who could play a number of different instruments. Mostly these talents seem to have been spent on amusing the children and sending them to sleep!

When Zwingli died, his lieutenant and successor, Heinrich Bullinger, took Anna and her two remaining young children into his own household.

the bomb bays of the Reformation in Zurich, making the Bible invasion almost impossible to resist.

Monasteries began shutting down: with monks and nuns simply leaving, or treating them like hotels, it was inevitable. Churches were transformed in every way: relics, images of saints, crucifixes, candles, altars and priestly robes were removed. Even organs were taken out, for Zwingli disapproved of instrumental music in church, fearing that its beauty would lure people to idolize music itself. But the real change came on Easter Day, 1525. Instead of celebrating Mass, plain bread rolls were placed on wooden plates on a simple table in the middle of the church; next to them was a jug of wine. No Latin was intoned; everything was in the Swiss German the people could understand. Then, for the first time, the people, while still seated in their pews, were given not only the bread but also the wine. And with that, no longer receiving the sacraments of the Roman church, the break with Rome was complete.

A sword for the Lord

In Zwingli's day, Zurich was a part of the Swiss confederation, officially part of the Holy Roman Empire, but to all intents and purposes an independent collection of mini-states (called cantons). Yet all this reformation of Zurich was making the more Catholic cantons increasingly nervous. Could the confederation survive religious disunity? Might the Catholic forces of the emperor make them all pay for Zurich's crime by invading? They preferred to pre-empt the sort of disasters they saw Zurich inevitably bringing down on them all. Soon, the war drums could be heard in the valleys, and in the summer of 1531, a comet (Halley's), portent of war, was seen in the heavens.

It didn't take long. A Swiss Catholic army was soon marching with one intent: to invade and convert Zurich. A defensive force was hastily mustered. Knowing that a successful attack would

The battle of Kappel

likely snuff out Zurich's gospel candle, Zwingli strapped on armour and prepared to lead the men. 'God's mercenary' to the last, he would defend the gospel with arms. On 11 October, outside Zurich at the battle of Kappel, the two armies locked horns. There was no contest: the forces of Zurich were easily smashed, and Zwingli himself badly wounded. Finding him unable to move, the victorious soldiers demanded that he pray to the Virgin Mary. He refused, and so Captain Fuckinger of Unterwalden stabbed him to death, leaving his men to quarter the body and burn it. As a final gesture, they then mixed his ashes with dung to prevent them ever being turned into a relic.

Very quickly a legend grew up around this. It was said that a symbolically important three days later, some friends found Zwingli's (presumably rather malodorous) remains on the battlefield. When they did so, they saw his heart emerge undefiled from the ashes. This they then divided up among themselves to be kept, most ironically, as relics. There is probably something more to the story than mere superstitious hokum, though. It is almost certain that before Zwingli was cut down he cried out 'You may kill the body but you cannot kill the soul!' What the legend of Zwingli's heart captures is that, while his body was struck down and burned, his heart could not be killed. His spirit lived on in those who had been touched by his preaching. The capable hands of Heinrich Bullinger took over the reins of Zurich's Reformation, guiding it into stable maturity over the next forty years. And, five years later, a Frenchman called John Calvin arrived in the Swiss city of Geneva, bringing with him, it would seem, a piece of Zwingli's heart.

Getting radical

Something both Luther and Zwingli faced was the presence of radicals. In both Wittenberg and Zurich there were those who thought that the Reformation was going too slowly, or not far enough. The story of the Radical Reformation really belongs most of all to Zurich, because it was radicals from there who, in the end, were overwhelmingly more successful. It was they who were to leave the most lasting legacy. However, first of all we need to return, briefly, to Wittenberg.

The year is 1521. Martin Luther, returning from the Diet of Worms, has been kidnapped and taken into protective custody in the Wartburg castle. The Reformation in Wittenberg is thus temporarily in the hands of Luther's colleague, Andreas Carlstadt. A mistake: Carlstadt was a hothead, pushing reform at a rate the people could not cope with. On Christmas Day, for example, he gave both bread and wine to the people, ordering them to take the bread from the plate themselves, rather than inserting it into their mouths as Catholic priests would. The people were shocked and terrified. They believed the bread was the very body of Christ: to pick it up with their dirty hands was horribly sacrilegious. One man was trembling so badly he dropped the bread. Carlstadt commanded him to pick it up, but by then the man was so over-come that he couldn't.

It was not just Carlstadt forcing fast-track reform. Once the evils of idolatry had been proclaimed from the pulpit, it was often near impossible to stop mobs from going on alcohol-fuelled shrine-smashing rampages. This isn't to deny the religious sincerity of the image-smashers. Many were deeply opposed to those images and all they stood for. The thing was, there wasn't much in the way of exciting recreation in the sixteenth century, but smashing up statues, breaking glass and burning wooden images was definitely fun. The drunk and the bored didn't need much to entice them. And the whole experience was often deliberately made funny. In one case, for example, a wooden statue of the Virgin Mary was accused of being a witch. It was thrown into the river to be tested. Being wood, of course, it floated, and thereupon it was condemned and burned. Everyone enjoyed that one.

On top of all that, three men from nearby Zwickau arrived in Wittenberg, claiming to be prophets who had no need of the Bible since the Lord spoke with them direct. They rejected infant baptism and advocated the speeding of the kingdom of God through the slaughter of the ungodly. 'Be born again or die!' The sluice-gates of change had been opened, and here was the white water. Wittenberg was spiralling into chaos.

Luther, ignoring the death-sentence that hung over him, came out of hiding to call for more careful reform. He preached a series of sermons in which he, like Zwingli, argued that true reform comes by the conversion of hearts, not the alteration of external practices. And, like Zwingli, he said that the power to change hearts is found only in the word of God, not in hammers, fire and force:

> I will constrain no man by force, for faith must come freely
> without compulsion. Take myself as an example. I opposed
> indulgences and all the papists, but never with force. I
> simply taught, preached, and wrote God's Word; otherwise
> I did nothing. And while I slept, or drank Wittenberg beer
> with my friends Philip and Amsdorf, the Word so greatly
> weakened the papacy that no prince or emperor ever
> inflicted such losses upon it. I did nothing; the Word did
> everything.

The radicals, Luther believed, had missed the point of the Reformation. His attack was on the idea that we could ever do anything to earn merit before God. Their attack was on external things like images, the sacraments and, in the case of the Zwickau 'prophets', the Bible. His message was that all salvation is a pure gift to be received with simple faith. Theirs was that external things must be rejected.

The twin tornadoes: Müntzer and Münster

If Luther was able to contain things in Wittenberg, elsewhere the fire was beginning to get out of control. As much as anything, this was because of Thomas Müntzer, a walking inferno who made Carlstadt look like a wet blanket. With his own unique blend of mysticism, Lutheranism and Islam, Müntzer was a hellfire-and-brimstone preacher who saw himself as a new Gideon, a warrior-prophet sent to bring judgment to the ungodly. All this he knew because, he believed, God spoke his 'inner word' directly to his heart, a word infinitely superior to the dead 'outer word' of the Bible that Luther banged on about. Unsurprisingly, he was not particularly polite about Luther, who he saw as an enemy of the real Reformation. Luther, of course, could give as good as he got: 'Müntzer,' he once said, 'thinks he has swallowed the Holy Spirit, feathers and all!'

Müntzer was passionately concerned to see the social implications of Luther's gospel. Luther had taught the spiritual equality and freedom of all believers. Müntzer thought that this should carry through into society to become social equality and political freedom. Inequality, political oppression and all ungodliness should be purged. Then the apocalypse would come, and Müntzer wanted to speed that day with the edge of his sword. All this ran right against the grain of Luther's own thought, who understood Christian freedom to be something entirely unconnected to political freedom. The famous opening statements of his *The*

Freedom of a Christian said it all: 'A Christian is a perfectly free lord of all, subject to none. A Christian is a perfectly dutiful servant of all, subject to all.' For Luther, the oppressed peasant could, spiritually, be just as free as the opulent prince.

Nevertheless, men like Müntzer and social unrest often come together. In 1381 it was John Ball's cry ('When Adam delved and Eve span, Who was then a gentleman?') that stoked the English Peasants' Revolt. History was about to repeat itself. Müntzer's fiery apocalyptic preaching was a blast of pure oxygen on the smouldering social discontent of the day. Soon much of Europe would be on fire. The times were certainly ripe for a man like Müntzer: the air was filled with apocalyptic expectations and wild prophecies. A prediction that in 1524 all the planets would align in the sign of Pisces was widely seen as presaging some great evil. Tensions then exploded into the German Peasants' War of 1524–5, the biggest popular revolt in Europe before the French Revolution of 1789. The climax came in 1525, when Müntzer led a peasant army to the battle of Frankenhausen. As fighting was about to commence, a rainbow appeared, which Müntzer interpreted as a sign of God's judgment on the enemy. The ill-equipped peasants charged in, only to be slaughtered by the professional army. Müntzer was caught, tortured and beheaded.

With him died much good will towards the Reformation. Many rulers, unable to distinguish between Müntzer and Luther, now became implacably hardened towards the movement as a whole. If Reformation meant rebellion, they were determined to crush it. As for those rulers who were able to make the distinction, their anger and suspicion was just as equally focused on all forms of radicalism. It would no longer be tolerated.

Yet Müntzer was just a first shot across Europe's bow. Worse was to come. A charismatic baker from Haarlem, Jan Matthijs, still believed with many others that the end was nigh. Unlike Müntzer, though, Matthijs knew the details. He predicted that the city of Münster in northwest Germany was the future new Jerusalem. It would be the centre of all the apocalyptic action, where the true believers would gather, and from where the judgment of Armageddon would begin. Radicals were soon flocking to Münster, where in 1534 they managed to come to power in the city council elections.

With that, change came instantly. Infant baptism was outlawed and adult baptism was made compulsory. Those who resisted were expelled from the city. Communism was enforced, with doors having to be left open day and night to show that all property really was held in common. Münster had become the scandal of Europe, and soon the city was put under siege. Yet that only fed the apocalyptic fervour inside. On Easter Sunday, 1535, Matthijs rushed out alone against the besieging army, apparently under the impression that God would enable him, single-handedly, to defeat them all. He did not. Perhaps a man called Jan van Leiden encouraged him in this, for he was the one who then succeeded Matthijs (having suitably impressed all Münster by running naked through the streets shouting ecstatic prophecies and foaming at the mouth).

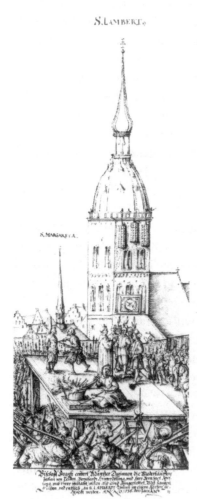

The execution of Jan van Leiden and his henchmen (note the three cages hanging from the tower).

Van Leiden dissolved the city council, chose a symbolic twelve new elders, and with a golden apple in his hand (representing his global rule) had himself anointed as the King David of this new Jerusalem. Polygamy was now instituted and enforced, execution being the alternative option. In fact, refusing adult baptism, complaining, backbiting, scolding one's parents and any number of trivial 'offences' now became punishable by death. Jan personally beheaded and trampled one of his sixteen wives in the town square merely for being cheeky.

Finally fed up with all this, in June 1535 two citizens opened one of the city gates to the besieging army (a combined Catholic-Lutheran force, such was the unity of opposition), who poured in to slaughter nearly everyone. But for van Leiden, only the most grisly death would do: he and two henchmen were torn apart with red-hot pincers and deposited in three cages, which (though the bones have long gone) can still be seen hanging from St Lambert's church tower.

Some (the Batenburgers, led by John of Batenburg) thought the problem was that Jan van Leiden had not been thorough enough. Keeping up his polygamous communism, they went on a rampage, killing all who would not join them. For the vast majority, though, the combined legacy of Müntzer and Münster cast a long shadow of suspicion over the Radical Reformation. With friends like that, radicals didn't need enemies. Pacifists many of them may have been, but all were now tarred as dangerous revolutionaries. It was to mean decades of savage persecution from all sides. It was also to mean a change of tack. Now made suspicious of charismatic self-proclaimed prophets, increasing numbers began turning to the more Bible- and peace-loving radicalism coming out of Zurich.

Sausagegate

In Zurich they didn't do revolts and rampages. They ate sausages. It was the Lent of 1522, when twelve friends got together to hold a sausage-eating party. Tradition had it that one was not supposed to eat meat during Lent. These men wanted to defy human tradition. Zwingli sat that one out: making gestures with sausages was not his way of reformation. But he did publicly defend his friends, for Lent, he argued, was just a human institution. Christians are to worship only according to God's command; to add human commands (about such things as what Christians can eat and when) was to add an unnecessary burden to people that Christ never asked his followers to bear.

However, the Zurich sausage scandal was just the first rumble. It showed there were men in Zurich who disagreed with Zwingli's model of reformation only through Bible teaching. Soon they were disrupting services and smashing images. More, they wanted to separate themselves from the corruption of the church they saw around them, setting up pure, new congregations, made up only of true believers. This was their other main disagreement with Zwingli. He wanted to reform the church, not leave it.

Together, these differences – wanting to force reformation, and wanting to separate – created the baptism crisis. In 1524, the pastor of a town near Zurich began preaching against infant baptism, and some began to refuse to have their children baptized. It was a clear statement that they wished to force their separation from the corrupt old church. And so, as the Lord's Supper split Luther from Zwingli, baptism would split Zwingli from the radicals. It was ironic, though, because in many ways the radicals' view of baptism was just an extension of Zwingli's own thought. Zwingli had argued that the Lord's Supper was about expressing one's faith. The radicals said it was the same with baptism. They saw baptism as a public testimony to the fact that inwardly they had already been baptized in the Spirit and born again. Yet this was very different to what Zwingli and Luther said about baptism. For them, baptism is an offering of the gospel corresponding to Old Testament circumcision, and is something to be responded to in faith. It made all the difference: what Zwingli and Luther said made it entirely appropriate to baptize infants. What the radicals said made it entirely wrong.

A public disputation on the subject was arranged in 1525. At the end, Zwingli and Bullinger were judged to have won the argument, and the council ordered all children to be baptized on pain of banishment. A few days later, a small group of men made their way through the snow to Felix Mantz's house. There, Conrad Grebel, the much-loved leader of the Zurich radicals, baptized George Blaurock, who then baptized the others himself. In the weeks that followed, many more adults were baptized, and they soon began celebrating the Lord's Supper for themselves. Everybody could recognize this as a declaration of independence from the existing church: this was now a distinct movement, the 'Swiss Brethren'. If people didn't immediately get the point, they would have done when a number of them paraded through Zurich crying 'Woe, woe to thee, Zurich!' Because they had received adult baptism on top of the baptism they had received as children, they (along with all radicals) were henceforth scathingly known as 'Anabaptists' (literally, 're-baptizers').[1]

All this was intolerable to the city council, who decreed that such re-baptizers should be sentenced to a second re-baptism by being drowned. The first to face this fate was Felix Mantz. In January 1527 he was taken out in a small boat into the middle of the River Limmat that runs through Zurich, his hands were tied and he was lowered into the icy water to drown. Those who stood on the banks and watched were struck by his quiet and gentle courage. They may have despised what he had stood for, but they were forced to acknowledge that here was a radical very unlike Thomas Müntzer.

In many ways, Mantz showed the future for Anabaptism: passive instead of aggressive, separatist instead of revolutionary, led by the Bible instead of the 'inner word'. Yet, like Mantz, Anabaptism could not expect better treatment as a result. The long shadows of Müntzer and Münster would dog them for more than a century, ensuring they remained the despised and feared bogeymen of Europe. Three more soon followed Mantz to the bottom of the River Limmat. They were just the first of a huge catalogue of Anabaptist martyrs.

If anything, rejection only encouraged the separatism of the Anabaptists. As the world rejected them and their message, so they would shake the dust from their sandals and reject the world. They would create a radically separate alternative society of dedicated disciples away from the corruption of the hostile world. Its sinful ways would be shunned, along with any who clung to them. Thus, for example, Jacob Hutter established a series of communist settlements in the relative outback of Moravia. In 1527 Michael Sattler met together with other Anabaptists in Schleitheim, to the north of Zurich, and there drew up what amounted to an Anabaptist confession of faith, the Schleitheim Confession. Its seven articles embodied separatism, as it affirmed believer's baptism; the need to shun the sinful; that the Lord's supper is only for baptized adult believers; the separation of believers from unbelievers; the importance of 'shepherds' in the church, and the people's right to choose them; complete pacifism; a rejection of oath-taking.

However, if any Anabaptists were naïve enough to imagine that their separatism might help them to be conveniently forgotten or left alone by the world, they would be badly disappointed. To the political authorities this separatism was almost as alarming as revolt. Not only did it offend by suggesting that nobody else was really Christian, but refusing to take an oath of allegiance to the state and not being prepared to fight for their country looked distinctly treasonous. Hutter and Sattler experienced what it would be like for so many who followed them: both were horribly tortured, and then Hutter was burned alive and Sattler torn apart with red hot pincers.

The other striking thing about the Schleitheim Confession, apart from its separatism, was how theologically light it was. Its seven articles are really concerned with practical questions, not who God is, or how we can be saved. And it seems that this was not just because they were trying to tackle the hot issues of the day; they actually reflect something important in the Anabaptist mentality. Anabaptism, on the whole, tended to be more interested in Christian living than theology. For the Magisterial Reformers[2] like Luther, theology came first, informing how we then live; for the Anabaptists, holiness came first, and theology was then done to spur on Christian obedience. Luther believed that this was a disastrous step backwards, for by failing to study

Menno Simons

Perhaps the greatest Anabaptist leader and advocate of these theological positions was the Dutchman, Menno Simons. Born thirteen years after Luther, like Luther he had started off as a Roman Catholic priest. Doubts began to set in, though, and, along with his brother Peter, he began to be attracted to the Anabaptist cause. In

Menno Simons (1496–1561)

1535, Peter was sucked into the Münster affair and killed. Menno was appalled, and wrote his first work, *The Blasphemy of Jan van Leyden*. It was a rallying call for pacifist Anabaptism, and Menno was to become its leader. Under his guidance, Anabaptism moved away from bloody revolutions and private revelations. The Mennonites were to be peaceful and biblical. Thus Menno sealed the victory of the Zurich Anabaptist martyr Felix Mantz's non-aggressive, biblical radicalism. Müntzer and Münster were to be ruins of the past; Menno gave Anabaptism a future.

the gospel of grace sufficiently, the Anabaptists were regressing into a religion of works. As a result he called them the 'new monks', for he believed that, like the old monks, they had separated themselves off from the world only to stare at their own spiritual navels.

Their theology was not just insubstantial, though. Separatism and the primacy given to Christian living combined to create theologies that often outrightly contradicted the essential thoughts of Protestantism. Luther's discovery of justification by faith alone, for example, was thought by most radicals to pose a serious danger to real Christian holiness, and was thus rejected. The same was true of his belief that we are all born enslaved to sin. If that were true, they wondered, why even try to be holy? Surely it is better to say that we become sinful only when we, personally, sin? And so, instead of our fate being determined by our union with either Adam or Christ, as Luther believed, salvation became more a matter of personal effort. It was more about imitating Christ than being saved by him. But then, they even radically reworked who Christ was. Those who sought at all costs to be unspotted by the world could not bear the thought that Christ might ever have been tainted by it. So, they argued, his body cannot have been of this world; his flesh came not from Mary but from heaven. That being the case, Christ never shared our humanity: he came, not to redeem humanity, but to show us an entirely different way.

Which to trust: Bible? Spirit? Reason?

Though historically all radicals got called Anabaptists, historians today tend to divide the Radical Reformation into three camps: the Anabaptists, the Spiritualists, and the Rationalists.

The first two we have already seen. The Anabaptists tended to see the Bible as their supreme authority, though they differed from the Magisterial Reformers in what they saw there. The

Spiritualists were men like Thomas Müntzer, who followed God's 'inner word' spoken directly to their heart. They scorned external things like the Bible and the sacraments. Sebastian Franck, for example, in his *The Book with Seven Seals* (1539), listed what he saw as all the contradictions in the Bible in order to turn readers from the dead and useless written word to the living inner word of the Spirit. Perhaps their most influential leading light was Caspar Schwenckfeld, who gathered a following of such loyalty that there are still Schwenckfelders today. How they used to meet was typically Spiritualist: with no ministry, no sacraments and no formal worship, they contented themselves with prayer and mutual exhortation in private homes.

We have not yet met the third group, the Rationalists. This group saw that the Reformation had proved the church had been wrong on many things. But, like the other radicals, they did not feel that the mainstream reformers had gone far enough. There were other traditional church beliefs, they saw, like the doctrine of the Trinity, that needed to be overthrown, just as much as purgatory, indulgences and the Mass.

The leading figure here was an Italian from Siena called Fausto Sozzini (1539–1604), or Faustus Socinus as he became better known. He developed the ideas of his uncle Lelio to create a system of thought, Socinianism, that was taken to be the most serious ideological threat of the seventeenth century by Protestants and Catholics alike. It wasn't that the Socinians ever became especially numerous; their numbers were similar to the Schwenkfelders, and even more tucked away, in Poland. But they touched a nerve, for the Socinians questioned not just what we know, but how we know it. In their opinion, reason, not the Bible, should be the judge, and nothing should be believed that contradicts 'sound reason' or contains a contradiction in itself. The Trinity was thus quickly shown the door (three can't be one), and, in complete contrast to the Anabaptist belief that Jesus wasn't really human, they argued that he wasn't really God. Getting rid of the Trinity had always been more popular at the edges of Europe, where there was more interaction with Jews and Muslims. Life there could be so much easier without the offence of the Trinity.

Of course, getting rid of the Triune God of Christianity meant getting rid of Christianity and finding a new God and a new religion, which is precisely what Socinianism did. In this religion, Jesus was just a teacher, not a saviour. The cross was no longer about sin being dealt with and forgiveness achieved. It was a simple, if moving, martyrdom. In fact, forgiveness for sins was hardly an issue, because the reality of divine judgment was denied. In other words, Socinianism sowed the seed of rational, moral, modern religiosity.

Clearly there were many different models of reformation, some a very far cry from Luther's! What made all the difference was neither zeal, nor strategy, nor hard work, but theology.

Notes

1   The Anabaptists should not be confused with the Baptists. Despite similarities and agreements, the Baptists are not directly descended from the Anabaptists, but have a different history, starting a century later in England.

2   The mainstream Reformers are often referred to as 'magisterial' Reformers because of their cooperation with secular magistrates.

4 After darkness, light: John Calvin

John Calvin could hardly have been more different from Luther and Zwingli. He was certainly not Zwingli's brawny soldier-type. A 'timid scholar', he called himself. Nor would he ever have enjoyed one of those raucous meals with the Luthers. Thin as a rake, Calvin was known as a 'great faster' who starved himself constantly. At the best of times he ate just one small meal a day so as to clear his mind and protect a body relentlessly besieged by ill-health. Where Luther would roar with laughter and gulp his beer, Calvin would much rather have sat quietly with his books. Where Luther was brash and earthy, Calvin was self-composed and (usually) polite. Both had eyes that people noticed, but where Luther's were said to twinkle, Calvin's burned. Both had tempers that could be fearsome when roused, but where Luther was hot, Calvin was cold. Both wrote huge quantities, but where Luther would fire off books like a semi-automatic in a street-fight, Calvin would spend years polishing and re-polishing his pièce de resistance.

Calvin could never have been a celebrity Christian: a camera-shy intellectual, he always avoided the limelight. His portraits show a thin face, that often-throbbing head covered with a simple black cap, and strikingly intense eyes. In that, they are quite revealing, for while pitifully weak in body, and naturally retiring by temperament, he was dauntingly strong in both mind and will. A lamb he was born, a lion he became for the Lord who saved him.

Renaissance

10 July 1509: Luther and Zwingli had just become priests, one terrified, the other itching for battle, and Jean Cauvin was born in the agricultural market town of Noyon, some sixty miles north of Paris. Cauvin was a Frenchman, and would always see France as his native land, and Noyon as his home on earth. But it was as 'Calvin' (the name sounded so much better in Latin) that he would lead the next generation of the Reformation.

Calvin was born just in time to know the world before there

John Calvin

was a Reformation. Growing up immersed in local church life and business, he later recalled kissing part of one of St Anne's bodies (she had many, scattered across Europe). Yet his start in life was the exact opposite of Luther's: his father actually intended him for the priesthood. Thus, aged about twelve, he was sent to Paris to study theology. For centuries, Paris had been the mother-ship of theological study in Europe, but Calvin's college would soon have a more surprising claim: within a few short years it produced as alumni Erasmus, the leader of moral church reform, Calvin, and Ignatius Loyola, the general of the Catholic Counter-Reformation. However, after about five years, Calvin's father abandoned the dream of priesthood for young Jean, withdrew him from Paris, and sent him instead to Orléans to study law. While Luther had infuriated his father by abandoning a career in law to become a priest, Calvin senior seems to have had a falling out with the church, and in any case, he was coming round to Luther senior's view that there were better prospects in law.

In Orléans, the young Calvin was plunged into the heady world of Renaissance humanism, and he loved it. Here was a community of scholars dedicated to the recovery of the classical beauties of Greece and Rome. Through their learning, they were going to bring about the rebirth of that golden age. It was exciting, yet it was also reassuringly comfortable. It involved critiquing the church, to be sure, but gently, from within. Attachment to the Virgin Mary and belief in purgatory were never questioned. Calvin threw himself into it, hoping that in a few years he could prove himself, and steal Erasmus' crown as the prince of the new learning.

However, there were some in Calvin's new social circle who knew more of the grace of Christ than Erasmus did. At least, Luther reckoned so. First, there was Calvin's cousin, Pierre Robert, nicknamed 'Olivétan' for his olive-oil study lamp that never seemed to be put out at night. Revealing a family tendency to almost incessant work, he managed to produce a complete translation of the Bible into French by the time he was twenty-nine. Then there was Melchior Wolmar, who taught Calvin Greek. That was an initiation into a much more edgy circle. By this time in the 1520s, Greek was the language of Reformation. The University of the Sorbonne in Paris, champion of the old orthodoxy, had seen clearly the dangers of Greek and Hebrew, and tried legal proceedings to stop what was an obvious open door to heresy. Presumptuous minds, armed with a knowledge of the biblical languages, might think they could understand the Scriptures for themselves merely by reading the text. However, the professors of the Sorbonne argued, the true meaning of Scripture is found in its 'mystical' sense, which no man can know 'unless he is educated in the faculty of theology'.

Perhaps Wolmar passed on more than his knowledge of Greek, perhaps he lent Calvin some copies of Luther's writings; at any rate, 'rebirth' began to mean something more personal to Calvin than the recovery of the classical age. As he later wrote, around this time 'God by a sudden conversion subdued and brought my mind to a teachable frame'. We know no more than that. It was characteristic of Calvin, who never liked to speak about himself. But, for all his desire to carry on his private life of scholarship, he had now become, as he put it, a 'lover of Jesus Christ'.

France on fire

Things had been looking positive for the Reformation in France. The young king, Francis I, was no stake-wielding zealot, but a humane, enlightened monarch, protective of those who spoke of reforming and purifying the church. Then, in 1528, someone took a knife to a prominent miracle-working statue of the Virgin Mary in Paris, decapitating the Madonna and child, smashing their heads and trampling on the canopy. Francis wept on hearing the news and led a procession through the streets to atone for the sin. It was exactly the sort of behaviour Luther had condemned in Wittenberg, and yet it was Luther's followers that would suffer for the outrage. Measures against any who even concealed Lutherans began to be set in motion. Added to this, the pope soon made a special plea to Francis, that he stamp out 'the Lutheran heresy and other sects infesting this kingdom'.

Then, in this more jumpy time, the new rector of the University of Paris, Nicholas Cop, opened the new term with an address that was just too Lutheran for comfort. With his arrest imminent, he fled the country and made his way to Basel in Switzerland, there to join the likes of Erasmus and other refugees like Olivétan.

Calvin's name was quickly black-listed. Perhaps he had had a hand in Cop's speech. The authorities came looking for him, and apparently he only made it out of his room in the nick of time, lowered out of the window on a rope of bed sheets. His room was ransacked, his correspondence seized, and now Calvin was on the run.

Then the temperature was turned up another notch. One October night, in 1534, placards attacking the Mass were posted in cities across France. One was even nailed to the door of the king's bedchamber in the Château d'Amboise. Nobody knew who had written them, but they were certainly not temperate. Calling themselves 'True Articles on the Horrible, Great and Important Abuses of the Papal Mass, Devised Directly Against the Lord's Supper of Jesus Christ', they railed against the blasphemous 'monkey business' and 'idolatry' of the Mass. If before it had not been clear in the king's mind, it was now: 'Reformation' was another word for dangerous sedition. He led another procession through Paris to atone for the sacrilege, only this time adding a new sacrifice to appease the offended Deity: along the procession route, pyres were lit to burn thirty-six offenders believed to have had a hand in the placards.

It all made life that much tenser for Calvin, trying to lie low. Though he agreed with the theology of the placards, Calvin was grieved by the hot-headed style of the placard-posters and the statue-knifers. Perhaps moved by this, he wrote his first work of theology, not against Rome, but against the Anabaptists. It gives an early sign of what would never leave his thinking: he hated those who, by perverting the Reformation or by their unbridled behaviour, gave the Reformation a bad name.

Before long, Calvin felt the situation in France had become intolerable. It had become an Egypt, a land of captivity that he had to leave so as to worship the Lord. And so, slipping across the border, Calvin became an exile. It was clearly a difficult decision, and he would never cease to look back longingly at his beautiful mother country, hoping that, one day, she might be

---

'Once for all'

The argument the placards used against the daily sacrifice of the Mass was Hebrews 7:27, 'Unlike the other high priests, he [Jesus] does not need to offer sacrifices day after day, first for his own sins, and then for the sins of the people. He sacrificed for their sins once for all when he offered himself.' If, in Germany, Romans 1:17 was the spark that had ignited the Reformation, in France, this was it. If Christ's sacrifice for sin on the cross was a complete work, and thus neither need be nor can be repeated, then all our attempts to atone for sin must be both unnecessary and insulting to Christ, in that they suggest his work is not sufficient. If Christ's sacrifice was indeed 'once for all', then there can be no need for other priests or high priests to offer up more. With that, the Mass, the priests who offered it, and all other acts of atonement for sin were shown to be useless. The only recourse was simple trust in Christ and his complete work.

---

freed. For that he would work: from exile he would call his Frenchmen to resistance.

'They went about . . . persecuted and ill-treated'

Calvin went first to Basel to join the likes of Cop and Olivétan. There, aged just twenty-six, and having had his 'sudden conversion' only a couple of years before, he completed the first edition of his life's work, the *Institutes of the Christian Religion*. He dedicated it to Francis I, who, after all, was known to be a thoughtful man, truly interested in church reform. He explained carefully to Francis that the Lutherans being persecuted were not, in fact, dangerous heretics, but were merely following the true Christian religion that the king had sworn to uphold. The work was about more than protecting evangelicals from persecution, however. His purpose, instead, he wrote, 'was solely to transmit certain rudiments by which those who are touched with any zeal for religion might be shaped to true godliness'. It was designed as a simple introduction to the evangelical faith ('*Institutes*' means 'basic instruction'). Published as a small book that could be hidden in a coat pocket, it was designed for the covert dissemination of the gospel. This was how Calvin hoped to bring the Reformation to France.

Business called him to sneak back briefly to Paris, from where he hoped to go and settle in Strasbourg, home to so many of the great minds of the Reformation. However, King Francis seemed to be constantly at war with Charles, the Holy Roman Emperor, and the Paris-Strasbourg road was at the time just where their armies were choosing to stare each other down. Calvin needed to skirt round them to the south, which meant passing through Geneva. Not a problem: an overnight stop by the beautiful lake, surrounded by the Alps, would make a lovely break in the journey.

Geneva was a city right on the borders of both France and the Holy Roman Empire, and there it had found the room to become, to all intents and purposes, almost entirely independent. And, in the last couple of years, it had been all change in Geneva. The Genevans had driven out their last bishop (a man who believed it the 'sovereign obligation of a prelate to set a full and dainty table, with good wines'); they had ceased the Mass, and told the priests either to convert or leave the city (most choosing the former). With that, Geneva officially allied herself to the Reformation. The city's motto had been *Post tenebras spero lucem* (After darkness I hope for light), but in commemoration of the event, coins were now struck with a new motto: *Post tenebras lux* (After darkness, light), for now, they declared, they had found what once they had hoped for.

The changes in the city were, of course, accompanied by the usual confusion, resistance, image-smashing and throwing of consecrated bread to dogs, and thus, when Calvin arrived, Geneva

Guillaume Farel

was in a state of considerable turmoil. They could do with some help getting started in the Reformation. Calvin had no intention of staying to help; however, the flame-haired and fiery Guillaume Farel, instigator of the Reformation in Geneva, heard that the author of the *Institutes* was in town, and he was not to be stopped. Just the sight of Farel at the door was probably scary enough for the young academic, twenty-one years his junior. Calvin managed to squeak something about going on to Strasbourg to pursue his studies, at which Farel

> proceeded to utter an imprecation that God would curse my retirement, and the tranquillity of the studies which I sought, if I should withdraw and refuse to give assistance, when the necessity was so urgent. By this imprecation I was so stricken with terror, that I desisted from the journey which I had undertaken.

And so, that summer of 1536, Calvin settled in Geneva to help Farel with the work of Reformation there. Poor Calvin! Yet Farel had picked his man wisely. They drafted a new confession of faith, and all who wished to remain in the city were ordered to accept it. They quickly made other proposals as well. Calvin wanted much more frequent Communion: instead of once a quarter, once a month. That might have been all right; the snag was, Calvin wanted notorious offenders to be denied access to Communion, and that would involve public humiliation in a community like Geneva's. Worse, it meant humiliation at the hands of a French immigrant. It was too much to be borne, and the city council eventually decreed that nobody could be refused the Lord's Supper.

The city had wanted Reformation, but not that much, and the more the Reformers started going about it, the more their relationship with the city council was strained. One of the preachers dared to list a few of the city's sins, referring to some of the Genevan magistrates as 'drunkards'. Such behaviour is, obviously, sheer madness for anyone who wants to be popular: he was swiftly imprisoned. Then Calvin and Farel were ordered to use the old-style wafer-bread that left no sacrilegious crumbs in Communion. They refused, and were thus banned from preaching. As if Calvin and Farel would stop preaching! Naturally, they both violated the ban, upon which they were given three days to leave the city. And so, in 1538, less than two years after arriving, Calvin found himself exiled once again.

Finding hope (and Mrs C)

On the one hand, Calvin was distraught: he felt he had failed as a reformer, and that his actions might yet push the Genevan church back to Rome. On the other hand, he was secretly glad: now he could go on to Strasbourg, as he had originally intended, and quietly settle down there with his books. They would be far less bother than those Genevans.

Poor Calvin! He was walking from Farel (who went his own way to Neuchâtel) straight into the arms of Martin Bucer, the leading reformer of Strasbourg. According to Luther, Bucer was

Martin Bucer

not only a 'blabbermouth', but also a wet. Calvin would gently concur that Bucer could, indeed, go on a bit, but when he arrived in Strasbourg, it was no namby-pamby that he met. When he told Bucer that he was just looking for a nice, hushed library, Bucer did a Farel on him, calling him a Jonah for fleeing from his calling, and insisting that he become the pastor of Strasbourg's French refugee church.

As it turned out, though, Calvin spent the happiest years of his life in Strasbourg. In stark contrast with Geneva, he found he was welcomed warmly by his fellow compatriots in exile. And then there was the happy fellowship: some of the main brains of the Reformation were there to chat to, and he enjoyed sharing his house with like-minded young evangelicals. There he learnt what a Reformation church could look like; there he experienced teaching at the Reformed college that had been started; there he got to write his first commentary (on Romans, naturally, given 'the chief point of the whole epistle, which is that we are justified by faith'). The only black cloud in this otherwise sunny period came when a theologian walked into town who had once (completely unfairly) accused Calvin of not believing in the Trinity. He revived the old charge, and Bucer summoned Calvin to answer for himself. Calvin went white with rage. He acquitted himself swiftly, but the accusation was so serious it would dog him for the rest of his life.

One cannot really speak of Calvin's romantic life. He was no Gallic paramour.

> As for marriage, I am not one of those infatuated lovers who, captivated by a pretty face, kiss even her vices. The only beauty which interests me is that she should be modest, obliging, not haughty, not extravagant, patient and solicitous for my health.

Nevertheless, he was keen to express his Protestant approval of marriage, and 1540 in Strasbourg became a whirl of match-making as his friends tried to help him find such a girl. It was

'Come home to Rome'

When Calvin and Farel were booted out of Geneva, many in Rome thought, like Calvin, that the city would turn back from the Reformation. Cardinal Sadoleto was one of them.

A charming, moderate and learned man, he felt that with a small shove in the right direction, prodigal Geneva would return. And so, with Calvin safely out of the way in Strasbourg, he wrote to the city of Geneva what was, effectively, a love-letter, wooing her back. It

Cardinal Jacopo Sadoleto

provides an illuminating insight into how Rome understood the Reformation.

His letter begins with a hearty verbal hug: 'Very dear brethren in Christ, Peace to you and with us, that is, with the Catholic Church, the mother of all, both us and you, love and concord from God'; and the rest of the letter is all honey and gush to the Genevans. The Reformers, of course, are those 'crafty men, enemies of Christian unity and peace' who had tried to lead the good Genevans astray. How? By teaching a false means of eternal salvation, something he urges the Genevans to think on seriously.

What is the truth, according to Sadoleto? Rome, he says, admits that 'we can be saved by faith alone' – a very surprising thing to hear from a cardinal! Then he clarifies:

'in this very faith love is essentially comprehended as the chief and primary cause of our salvation.' So, for Sadoleto, salvation by faith alone really means salvation by our own love.

But then, why trust Rome rather than the Reformers? For Sadoleto, the choice is simple: follow 'what the Catholic Church throughout the whole world, now for more than fifteen hundred years . . . approves with general consent; or innovations introduced within these twenty-five years'.

Just in case the Genevans have not already been won over, he then dramatically imagines an evangelical and a Catholic 'before the dread tribunal of the Sovereign Judge'. What would each say on that day, and who would be acquitted? The Catholic gets to speak to the judge first, and his defence is: '[I am] obedient to the Catholic Church, and revere and observe its laws, admonitions, and decrees.' Then the evangelical brazenly steps up and announces his defence, that evangelicals have shaken off 'the tyrannical yoke of the Church'. To what end? In order that 'trusting to this our faith in thee, [we] might thereafter be able to do, with greater freedom, whatsoever we listed'. (This particular 'evangelical' had clearly taken 'justification by faith alone' to mean that he should trust in his own act of faith, rather than in Christ – leaving Christ out of it clearly helped him feel free to live a life of self-indulgence.)

Unsurprisingly, the Catholic wins, and is taken into eternal bliss, while the evangelical is flicked into outer darkness. The reason is that the Catholic has trusted the church, which 'cannot err', while the evangelical has been 'trusting to his own head'. Again, it is clear that to Sadoleto's mind, if someone is not trusting in the church for his salvation, he must be trusting in himself. And so he asks of the evangelical: 'to what does he look as the haven of his fortunes? in what bulwark does he confide? to whom does he trust as his advocate with God?' It never seems to have entered his mind that the answer might be Christ.

And with one last parting shot at the Reformers – that they could not be speaking Christ's truth since they had divided the church – Sadoleto blesses his 'dearest brethren' and signs off.

With breath-taking cheek, considering how they had treated him, the Genevans asked Calvin to write a response for them. He agreed, and in six days produced a model apologetic for the Reformation.

Calvin's response opens with a genuine show of respect for Sadoleto as a man of learning; yet within a few short lines the claws come out, and Calvin sets about the total devastation of the cardinal's argument. First he pounces on Sadoleto's silky tone: 'it is somewhat suspicious', he writes, 'that a stranger, who never before had any intercourse with the Genevese, should now suddenly profess for them so great an affection, though no previous sign of it existed.'

Then, on to the content. Calvin makes it quite clear that the Reformers are not about dividing the church, but reforming it. And this reform is not their own innovation; instead, he argues, 'not only that our agreement with antiquity is far closer than yours, but that all we have attempted has been to renew that ancient form of the Church'. (The Reformers were always emphatic on that point.) As for the good Catholic's defence at the last judgment: 'the safety of that man hangs by a thread whose defense turns wholly on this – that he has constantly adhered to the religion handed down to him from his forefathers. At this rate, Jews, and Turks, and Saracens, would escape the judgment of God.'

The bulk of Calvin's response, though, is devoted to 'justification by faith, the first and keenest subject of controversy between us'. The way Calvin argues here is very revealing: 'Wherever the knowledge of it is taken away, the glory of Christ is extinguished.' In the Reformation mindset, salvation is a gift of God's grace alone (*sola gratia*), found, not in any pope or Mass, but in Christ alone (*solus Christus*), and received by simple faith alone (*sola fide*). And we can know this for certain only through Scripture (*sola Scriptura*). Only if all these things are true, the sinner contributing nothing to his own salvation, can all the glory go to God. Reformation thinking therefore had this as its guiding light for all theology: does the theology lead one to say 'to God alone be the glory' (*soli Deo gloria*), or does man retain some of the glory for himself? Sadoleto's problem, said Calvin, was exactly this: 'if the blood of Christ alone is uniformly set forth as purchasing satisfaction, reconciliation, and ablution, how dare you presume to transfer so great an honor to your works?' Sadoleto's half-baked idea of a salvation that was the fruit of both God's grace and man's love was actually a blasphemous denigration of Christ's cross and glory.

As for the charge that such gratuitous mercy would leave Christians without a care for living a holy life, Calvin deftly shows that it too forgets Christ: 'Wherever, therefore, that righteousness of faith, which we maintain to be gratuitous, is, there too Christ is, and where Christ is, there too is the Spirit of holiness, who regenerates the soul to newness of life.'

hard going: the first candidate did not speak French, another was not interested, another got as far as engagement before that had to be broken off. And all this by June! Two months later he was married to Idelette de Bure, a widow he had converted from Anabaptism (a conversion essential to domestic happiness in the Calvin household). She brought with her two children from her former husband (also Jean).

The marriage was not destined for bliss: 'out of fear that our marriage would be too happy, the Lord from the beginning moderated our joy' by sending an illness on them. Two years later, Idelette bore Calvin a son, Jacques. However, he was born prematurely, and only survived two weeks. Calvin wrote to a friend, 'The Lord has certainly inflicted a severe and bitter wound in the death of our baby son. But He is Himself a Father and knows best what is good for his children.' Idelette herself struggled to recover her health, and spent the last years of their marriage dying slowly. When at last she did die in 1549, leaving Calvin to care for her two children, the pain was transparent: 'I struggle as best I can to overcome my grief . . . I have lost the best companion of my life.' A natural romantic he had not been, but that never prevented Calvin from feeling and loving deeply.

Back into the fray

While Calvin was in happy exile in Strasbourg, Geneva was a mess. The author of the French placards attacking the Mass had come and gone as a pastor, there was doctrinal confusion, and there was political mayhem. Eventually the politics changed enough for Geneva to want Calvin back, and so, three years after coldly expelling him, they sent him a warm invitation to return. He would have laughed it off if he could; as it was, the thought of returning was just too horrible to think about. When urged to accept by Farel (who was, himself, too busy to return), he replied that he would prefer 'a hundred deaths to this cross'.

Yet with Bucer and Farel ganging up on him, he was eventually persuaded. Poor Calvin! In 1541, he returned to Geneva with Idelette and her children, and climbed the steep little Rue des Chanoines, where the city had provided him with a small, furnished house. With a little back-garden and a stunning view of the Alps, it was the city's sweetener; yet Calvin would never trust the Genevans again. He lived ever after out of a suitcase, as it were, ready to be ejected once more.

The air was thick with anticipation when he first climbed back into his old pulpit. The congregation braced themselves for the torrent of anathemas that must surely come from an embittered deportee now given a public voice. Instead, Calvin simply took up the exposition of the verse he had got to the last time he was there, three-and-a-half years before. The message was as clear as could be: Calvin had returned with no personal agenda (far from it!), but had come as a preacher of God's word.

However, if God's word really was going to be the sceptre by which God ruled his church in Geneva, something would have to be done to ensure that. The problem was that the city council had effectively grabbed for itself the power of the pope, and exercised, in a very 'hands-on' way, a control over everything that went on in the church. Calvin knew he had to strike while he was still welcome. And so, on the very day of his return, he submitted to the city council a list of proposals for the comprehensive reformation of the church in Geneva. Most were accepted.

A letter from Calvin to King Edward VI of England

The proposals made it very clear that Reformation was not about simply breaking from Rome; it meant dedication to ongoing reform by the word. The reformed church must be always reforming. Calvin proposed, among other things, that every household should receive a pastoral visit every year; that everyone should learn the catechism that explained the evangelical faith; and that only those who did so should be allowed to the Lord's Table. And, to make absolutely certain that Geneva could never be spoken of in the same breath as Jan van Leiden's polygamous commune of Münster, he proposed that a disciplinary committee be set up to ensure an orderly society.

The committee had no actual power to enforce discipline, and, once set up, for the most part it simply doled out verbal slaps on the wrist to those who skived sermons or catechism classes. It was known to be rather heavy-handed, though. In amusing contrast to Luther's Wittenberg, it tried banning citizens from frequenting taverns, providing them instead with 'abbeys', where they would be put under supervision with a French Bible. Unsurprisingly, the plan was not a great success. And, when a list was drawn up, pronouncing which Christian names were acceptable (like 'Jacques' and 'Jean'), and which unacceptable (like 'Claude' and 'Monet'), some began to feel that too much was being prescribed. Quite simply, many Genevans did not like being told to live the holy life of the committed when they themselves were not committed. 'Oh, we do not want this Gospel here, go look for another one', Calvin once accused the Genevans of saying. One can almost hear the whine in their voice.

It was all this that earned Calvin his reputation as the Protestant ayatollah. But that was always unfair. The man cannot be judged by the city. He was, as he said, a 'timid scholar' with no desire for despotic power, and no chance of ever having it. Being a refugee Frenchman, not a citizen of Geneva, he had no right to vote or hold any secular office, and he lived in the city only by the daily grace of the council, who could, on a whim, and at any time, expel him again.

Nevertheless, the very fact that he was an immigrant helped fuel resentment against Calvin as the figurehead of all reform. The situation was not helped by the huge tide of immigrants that was sweeping into Geneva, especially from France. When Calvin returned to the city in 1541, Geneva had a population of about 10,000, but by the end of his life, that had more than doubled. The newcomers were mostly French refugees, like Calvin, who transformed the city, introducing industries like clock-making, and even changing the main language spoken on the street to French.

One gets a sense of the appeal Geneva held to badgered evangelicals in France from what one woman from Calvin's birth-town of Noyon said on arrival:

> Oh, I am joyful at having left that accursed Babylonian captivity and that I am going to be delivered from my final prison! Alas, how it would be if I were now in Noyon, where I would not dare open my mouth to confess my faith frankly, even while the priests and monks vomited out all their blasphemies around me! And here I not only have liberty to give glory to my Saviour as to appear boldly before him, but I am guided there.

People were leaving behind whole livelihoods so as to come and live openly as evangelicals, and hear the Scriptures taught.

Yet, while the immigrants may have been happy, their arrival stoked the usual xenophobia, and taverns were full of what should be done with them. One popular idea was that they should 'take a boat and put all the Frenchmen and banished people in it to send them down the Rhone' back to France. Calvin's name was implied.

Things started getting ugly. A group of women was arrested for being caught dancing, provoking a savage back-lash against Calvin in which unrepeatably rude posters about him were plastered around the city, one even on Calvin's pulpit. It was an omen of worse to come, as the early 1550s saw riots and mounting tension, led by a party who loved parties and hated Calvin. During his sermons, people began to try drowning him out, some by coughing, others by making rude noises with their seats.

It all looked like Calvin was not going to survive much longer in Geneva. In 1553 he illegally declared that he would not allow one of the leading figures of this anti-Calvin, 'libertine' faction to the Lord's Supper. Fully expecting the next Sunday to be his last, he preached with a lump in his throat, and yet still refused to give in. Standing at the Lord's Table he announced, 'I will die sooner than this hand shall stretch forth the sacred things of the Lord to those who have been judged despisers.' Almost inexplicably, Calvin was not expelled. But his life in the city hung by a thread.

Michael Servetus

It was at this darkest hour that the event occurred which would cast the worst shadow over Calvin's name: Michael Servetus was burned for heresy in Geneva. The image of Calvin standing by the pyre, a grim smile on his face, certainly provides good fuel for the 'Calvin as Protestant Inquisitor' legend. So, what did happen? Is the monster revealed at last?

Michael Servetus

Michael Servetus was a Spanish radical of Faustus Socinus's ilk, who longed for the Reformation to press on and reject what he saw as other corrupt beliefs, like the Trinity. For centuries, Spain had had large Jewish and Muslim populations, and many Spanish Christians felt the Trinity was just an obstacle, keeping Christians out of a happy Spanish monotheism club. Servetus became the voice of that movement, arguing that the Trinity was a later belief added on to the simple, no-frills monotheism of Old Testament religion, where God the Father was God alone. If we could all just go back to that basic and original truth, then Jews and Christians need no longer be divided.

Catholics and Protestants alike were horrified by this espousal of an entirely different god. However, the Catholics caught him first, just over the French border from Geneva, in Vienne. Having found him guilty of heresy, they also managed to burn him first – though only in effigy, since by then he had escaped over the rooftops and over the border to Geneva.

Calvin was so hated there, it seemed like a good place for him to go. Even when he was arrested on sight he was optimistic: from prison he wrote to the city council, demanding Calvin's arrest and charitably offering to take Calvin's house and goods when Calvin was executed. In 1553, such requests seemed realistic. However, Geneva herself was accused by all Catholic Europe of being a harbour for heretics; even the city council could see that if they tolerated Servetus it would prove Rome right.

They summoned their theologian, Calvin, to act as their prosecutor. As expected, Servetus was found guilty, and in agreement with other Protestant cities in Switzerland and Germany, Geneva pronounced the sentence of death. This was no big deal: all Christendom agreed that death was the appropriate sentence for heresy, and in the decades beforehand, scores of self-confessed sorcerers, plague-spreaders and devil-worshippers (self-confessed while their feet were being grilled, of course) had been tortured and burned in Geneva. This was the sixteenth century.

It was also 1553, and Calvin was in no position whatsoever to influence the sentencing. In fact, he asked for a more lenient sentence of death by beheading, which was refused. He then went to see Servetus in prison one last time to try to win him over. He failed, and so Servetus was taken to the city gate and burned.

As the flames rose, Servetus cried 'Oh Jesus, son of eternal God, have pity on me!' Had he been prepared to cry 'Oh Jesus, eternal Son of God' he would never have been burned. It is disturbing in what that reveals. The two confessions are poles apart; but the fact that today we struggle to see that only displays how totally the doctrine-light spirit of Erasmus has conquered.

The tide turns

In 1555, it was as if the clouds suddenly cleared and the sun shone again. Those who favoured Calvin won the elections to the city council. This sparked a riot. Swords were drawn, and the leader of the old anti-Calvin party seized the city's baton of authority. There could have been no clearer symbol of a coup d'état. Then everyone remembered that such things do not happen in respectable Swiss cities, and the ring-leaders were condemned to be decapitated, nailed to the gibbet and quartered. Most managed to flee with their heads before they could be caught, but it had changed everything. It was a new era, the anti-Calvin party was well and truly out, and it would give Calvin the freedom to do things he had never ventured before.

What would Calvin do with this newfound opportunity? He established a top-secret programme for the evangelization of his native France. He was already well-established as the leader-in-exile of French Protestantism, in regular contact with many of the underground churches there. But after 1555, his efforts could be taken to a much more ambitious level. A secret network was set up, with safe houses and hiding places arranged, so that agents of the gospel could be slipped across the border into France to plant new, underground (sometimes literally) churches. With secret printing presses installed in Paris and Lyons to resource them, it was a stunning success. Demand for the literature soon far outstripped what the presses could supply, and printing became the dominant industry in Geneva in an attempt to cope with the need.

More than 10% of the entire population of France became Reformed, with some two million or more gathering in the

The St Bartholomew's Day massacre

 Calvin never lived to see it, but eight years after his death, on 24 August 1572 (St Bartholomew's Day), several leading Protestant aristocrats were assassinated in Paris. It was the culmination of an increasing tension between Protestant and Catholic factions of the French nobility over the religious future of the country. As had been intended, it sparked off a general massacre in Paris in which thousands of Protestants were killed by mobs. The violence quickly spread through France, and over the next few weeks, many more thousands were killed, and thousands more fled the kingdom. It was the sharpest and bloodiest check to Calvin's hopes for France.

hundreds of churches that were planted. Calvinism fared especially well among the nobility, roughly a third of whom appear to have converted, giving the Reformed faith a political clout disproportionate to its actual size. Calvin's long-held dream of an evangelical France began to look like a real possibility. He wrote a confession of faith for the church there, and supported them in whatever way he could. Despite the growth of evangelicalism in France, encouragement was desperately needed: when, for example, one church was raided in Paris, more than a hundred were arrested and seven burned. And, while he wrote to fortify them from a position of freedom, he never spoke as though from an ivory tower. His letters are splattered everywhere with mentions of the blood he was sure he would soon have to shed as, in Geneva, he felt the imminent threat of martyrdom: 'It is true that at this time I speak from outside the battle, but not very far, and I do not know for how long, since as far as one can judge our turn is indeed near.'

It was not just France. Calvin quite deliberately turned Geneva into an international centre for the propagation of the gospel. He advised Protestant rulers from Scotland to Italy, trained refugees who came to Geneva and then returned to their native

Calvin's academy

countries, and dispatched missionaries to Poland, Hungary, the Netherlands, Italy, even South America. The real engine-room for all this was the college and academy that Calvin opened in 1559. Starting with a general education and moving on to a detailed study of theology and books of the Bible, it equipped the pastors, who could then be dispatched, fully armed and trained, from Geneva.

Calvin devoted more of his time, though, to preaching and teaching. Lecturing three times a week, preaching twice each Sunday and, on alternate weeks, every weekday as well, this was for him the heart of the Reformation, as it was for both Luther and Zwingli. He also managed (mostly by putting his lectures together) to write commentaries on nearly every book of the Bible, so as to help preachers elsewhere. And these were a very different sort of commentary from what Europe had known before: their aim was 'an easy brevity that does not involve obscurity'. As a result of his 'sudden conversion', Calvin had become convinced that God brings life and new life into being only through his word, and so proclaiming that had become the essence of Calvin's life's work.

From Calvin to Calvinism

Calvin never intended to found something called 'Calvinism', and he hated the word. He spent his life fighting for what he believed was the mere orthodoxy of the early post-apostolic church, whereas the word 'Calvinism' suggested some new school of thought. However, something called 'Calvinism' did come into being, and its story would lead many to misunderstand the man himself. As a result, one of the most popular images of Calvin today is that of a man obsessed with God's election of who will and who will not be saved.

The difficulty really began with a Dutch student, Jacobus Arminius, who trained to be a pastor at the academy in

Geneva some twenty years after Calvin died.

Returning to Amsterdam, he began teaching some rather different things from what Calvin had taught, especially regarding predestination. His view was that God predestines people for salvation on the basis of his foreknowledge of their faith (rather than on the basis of his own divine will, as Calvin

Jacobus Arminius

taught). After he died in 1609, his followers (the 'Arminians') put together the Remonstrance, a petition that five of his core views be accepted in the Dutch Reformed Church.

In 1618–19, a synod of Reformed theologians met in Dordt (or Dordrecht) to deal finally with the Remonstrance. In response to its five points they produced their 'Five Articles against the Remonstrants', later put into the appropriately Dutch acronym 'TULIP':

T   **Total depravity**. Meaning not that we are as sinful as we possibly could be, but that sin has so comprehensively affected us that we have no ability to do anything towards our own salvation.

U   **Unconditional election**. Meaning that God unconditionally chooses some people for salvation and others for damnation, and does not base that decision on anything within those people, whether good or bad.

L **Limited atonement**. Meaning that, on the cross, Christ paid for the sins of the elect only, not for the sins of all humanity.

I **Irresistible grace**. Meaning that, when God intends to save a person, that person will be unable to resist and refuse to be born again.

P **Perseverance of the saints**. Meaning that God preserves true Christians to the end, never letting them 'fall away' from salvation.

While these 'five points of Calvinism' reveal a growing interest in predestination among Calvinists, they were drawn up to protect what the Calvinists believed were important truths denied by the Arminians. They were never intended to be a summary of Calvinist belief or Calvin's own thought.

The proof? In 1559, Calvin came out with his last, and grandest, edition of his *Institutes*. It was now way more than a handy entrée to the evangelical faith, as the first edition had been back in 1536. It had been worked up into a sumptuous, four-course banquet of gospel explanation, representing the richness and span of Calvin's thinking. If anything gives the lie to the idea of Calvin as a predestination-obsessive, it is this. After having looked at God, the world, all that Jesus has done for us, our salvation, prayer, and a number of other topics, it is only on page 920 of the standard version of the *Institutes* that Calvin starts looking at election – and, out of a whopping total of 1,521 pages, he only gives the topic 67 of them! Clearly, he did not have tunnel vision on predestination. His thought was rich and wide-ranging. It was an attempt to look at all things through the spectacles of God's word.

'To this day no-one knows where his grave is'

While 1555 marked an upturn in Calvin's ability to push the Reformation forward, it marked a downturn in his health from which he would never recover. Working with the ferocious energy that his extraordinary output demanded ravaged his fragile constitution. 'The affliction of my body has almost stupefied my mind', he confessed. And no wonder: a few months before his death he wrote to his doctors,

at that time I was not attacked by arthritic pains, knew nothing of the stone or the gravel – I was not tormented with the gripings of the cholic, nor afflicted with hemorrhoids, nor threatened with expectoration of blood. At present all these ailments as it were in troops assail me. As soon as I recovered from a quartan ague, I was seized with severe and acute pains in the calves of my legs, which after being partially relieved returned a second and a third time. At last they degenerated into a disease in my articulations, which spread from my feet to my knees. An ulcer in the hemorrhoid veins long caused me excruciating sufferings, and intestinal ascarides subjected me to painful titillations, though I am now relieved from this vermicular disease, but immediately after in the course of last summer I had an attack of nephritis. As I could not endure the jolting motion of horseback, I was conveyed into the country in a litter. On my return I wished to accomplish a part of the journey on foot. I had scarcely proceeded a mile when I was obliged to repose myself, in consequence of lassitude in the reins. And then to my surprise I discovered that I discharged blood instead of urine. As soon as I got home I took to bed. The nephritis gave me exquisite pain, from which I only obtained a partial relief by the application of remedies. At length not without the most painful strainings I ejected a calculus which in some degree mitigated my sufferings, but such was its size, that it lacerated the urinary canal and a copious discharge of blood followed. This hemorrhage could only be arrested by an injection of milk through a syringe. After that I ejected several others, and the oppressive numbness of the reins is a sufficient symptom that there still exist there some remains of uric calculus. It is a fortunate thing, however, that minute or at least moderately sized particles still continue to be emitted. My sedentary way of life to which I am condemned by the gout in my feet precludes all hopes of a cure. I am also prevented from taking exercise on horseback by my hemorrhoids. Add to my other complaints that whatever nourishment I take imperfectly digested turns into phlegm, which by its density sticks like paste to my stomach.

The end to his decade of pain came in 1564. Sensing his imminent death, he made his will, confessing 'I have no other defense or refuge for salvation than his [God's] gratuitous adoption, on which alone my salvation depends'. Confined increasingly to his bed, he asked all the pastors of Geneva to visit him one last time, imploring them, 'Brethren, after I am dead, persist in this work, and be not dispirited'. Finally, his body 'so emaciated that nothing seemed left but the spirit', he died in bed on 27 May. His protégé, Thèodore de Bèze (or Beza), felt the gravity of the moment, describing how 'at the same time with the setting sun, this splendid luminary was withdrawn from us'.

Since he had had no desire to become a relic or an idol, Calvin had requested that he be buried in the common cemetery in an unmarked grave. No glamour, no gravestone; it was typical Calvin.

5 Burning passion: the Reformation in Britain

'One little word shall fell him'

As in Wittenberg with Luther, as in Glarus with Zwingli, it was Erasmus' New Testament that started it all in Britain. Before long, a young priest called Thomas Bilney had read it and come across the words 'Christ Jesus came into the world to save sinners'. Previously he had despaired of his sins, but with these words, he said,

> immediately I seemed unto myself inwardly to feel a marvellous comfort and quietness, insomuch that my bruised bones leaped for joy. After this, the Scripture began to be more pleasant unto me than the honey or the honey-comb; wherein I learned that all my travails, all my fasting and watching, all the redemption of masses and pardons, being done without truth in Christ, who alone saveth his people from their sins; these, I say, I learned to be nothing else but even (as St. Augustine saith) a hasty and swift running out of the right way; or else much like to the vesture made of fig leaves, wherewithal Adam and Eve went about in

vain to cover themselves, and could never obtain quietness and rest, until they believed in the promise of God, that Christ, the seed of the woman, should tread upon the serpent's head.

Bilney was no Lutheran (he had come to his views quite independently), but until he was burned for his preaching in 1531, he was instrumental in drawing a number of others to the Reformation.

At the same time, Luther's books started pouring into the country, where they were welcomed by John Wycliffe's followers, the Lollards, who were as alive and active as ever. Of course, as soon as Luther had been condemned by the pope, his books were burned in Cambridge, Oxford and London; yet burning and banning books only ever seems to increase their popularity. And so it was: Lutheran books were smuggled in through ports like Ipswich, fuelling the spread of a network of underground Lutheran groups. In Cambridge, one group of dons was known to gather at the White Horse Inn, where all the Luther-talk and beer made it look so like Wittenberg that it was soon nicknamed 'Little Germany'.

William Tyndale

Meanwhile, over in the rural west of England (Little Sodbury in Gloucestershire, to be precise), a brilliant young linguist called William Tyndale was beginning to cause ructions at the home of his employer, Sir John Walsh. He was only there to be tutor to Sir John's children, but he had spent so much time with Erasmus' New Testament that his dinner-table conversation could put even the strongest Catholic stomachs off their food. One scholar was so exasperated with Tyndale that he blurted out

'We were better be without God's law than the pope's'. Tyndale replied, 'I defy the pope, and all his laws,' adding, 'and if God spare my life, ere many years I will cause a boy that driveth the plough shall know more of the Scripture than thou dost.'

It was no idle boast. Tyndale set about his life's work of translating the Bible from its original Greek and Hebrew into English. He sailed for Germany, making his way to Worms; and there, where just five years earlier Luther had made his 'Here I stand' speech in front of the Emperor, Tyndale published his complete New Testament in English. For over a hundred years, the followers of John Wycliffe had produced and read translations of the New Testament in English, but they were only hand-written, rather wooden renditions of the Latin Vulgate. They were impossible to mass-produce, and still contained all the theological problems of the Latin ('do penance' instead of 'repent', for example). Tyndale's New Testament, however, could and would be printed off by the thousands, then smuggled into England in bales of cloth, and soon accompanied by his *Parable of the Wicked Mammon*, an argument for justification by faith alone. Even more importantly, Tyndale's New Testament was a gem of a translation. Accurate and beautifully written, it was a page-turner.

None of which impressed the English bishops. To them, Tyndale's work was just plain dangerous, and all copies that could be found were burned, along with their owners. And, bluntly, the bishops were right: Tyndale's translation was highly dangerous. 'Do penance' in the Vulgate was now 'repent' in Tyndale's version; 'priest' was merely 'senior', 'church' just 'congregation', 'confess' now simply 'acknowledge', 'charity' now 'love'. It pulled the biblical carpet right out from under the claims of the church. How to be saved and what being a Christian meant looked completely different: in place of all formal, external sacramentalism was a call for a change of heart.

Eventually the wrath of the church caught up with Tyndale, but not before he had managed to translate a good portion of the Old Testament, and some 16,000 copies of his Bible had been

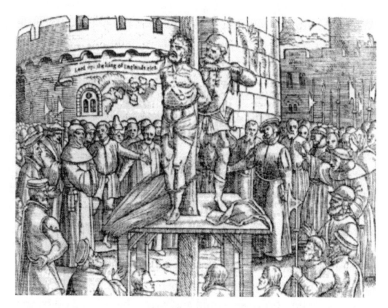

Tyndale's execution

smuggled into England. It was an incredible feat at a time when there was a largely illiterate population of at most 2.5 million. In 1535 he was caught, and the following October he was officially strangled and burned near Brussels, uttering the immortal last words 'Lord, open the King of England's eyes!'

Dynasty: a soap opera

That 'King of England' was Henry VIII, and whether or not Tyndale's prayer was answered precisely, he would transform England from a devotedly Roman Catholic nation to one where the Bible was read, preached and discussed in English.

Henry was an autocratic ruler with a fearsome, often lethal, temper and energy like a coiled spring (and not much more predictability). He was also deeply religious: he would serve the priest at Mass himself (attending at least three masses a day), and for his adamant support of the pope he was awarded the Golden

Rose, just like Luther's prince, Frederick the Wise. It was unsurprising, then, that he opposed Luther when he heard of him. In 1521, with the help of a few willing ghost-writers, he even penned a polemic against Luther entitled *A Defence of the Seven Sacraments*, dedicating it to the pope. For this, the pope awarded him with what would become a most ironic title: 'Defender of the Faith'. We shouldn't be too impressed: all the major rulers of the day 'bore titles indicating their devotion to the Prince of Peace. Francis was the *Most Christian King of France*, Charles *His Most Catholic Majesty* of Spain, Henry was called *The Defender of the Faith*, and Leo [the Pope], of course, the *Vicar of Christ*. Their conduct already belied too sanguine a hope. Henry, for his campaign against France in 1513, had cast twelve great guns, each named for one of the apostles, who were to belch fire against the Most Christian King.'[1] Nevertheless, the 'Defender of the Faith' was hardly a bright hope for the Reformation.

Then he hit problems with his marriage. Aged seventeen, Henry had been rather reluctantly married to his elder brother's widow, Catherine of Aragon. After a few years of numerous miscarriages and babies dying soon after birth, it became clear to Henry that Catherine was incapable of providing him with an heir. She had borne him a daughter (Mary) in 1516, but that was not much good to Henry. England had just got through the Wars of the Roses, in which the succession had been disputed. Henry wanted a son to avoid any possibility of a re-run. The obvious solution was to get another wife, one who could deliver. The usual form for men in Henry's situation was to find a fault that made the marriage illegal and then get it annulled. Henry didn't have to look hard: Leviticus 20:21 states 'If a man marries his brother's wife, it is an act of impurity; he has dishonoured his brother. They will be childless.' (And Henry considered he was childless: it was proof that his marriage was illicit.) The reason Henry knew the verse was because it was the very thing that had been a problem when he had married his brother's widow in the first place. However, back then, Pope

Julius II had very obligingly removed the scriptural prohibition with a special dispensation.

Henry needed to get the new pope, Clement VII, to undo the dispensation. It raised a mighty question: while Julius clearly believed he could nullify scriptural commands, could a pope nullify the dispensations of a previous pope? Usually, the cogs of church law could be oiled to accommodate powerful kings like Henry. The problem was Catherine herself. She insisted that her first marriage had never been consummated, meaning that the papal dispensation had never been necessary in the first place, her marriage to Henry being straightforwardly legitimate. Other women could have been steamrollered into submission. However, Catherine's nephew was Emperor Charles V, who had already sacked Rome and imprisoned Clement VII once. Charles was not going to allow his aunt to be cast aside, and there was no way the pope was going to antagonize an emperor who could well sack Rome again. And so the pope could not clear the way to annulling Henry's awkward marriage.

Henry, however, was not so easily stopped. In fact, quite the opposite: when his eye fell on the fascinating and nubile young Anne Boleyn, he became relentless in his bid to switch Catherine for her. First he tried diplomatic pressure on the pope, then squeezing the English clergy in the hope that the pope might crack. At the same time he set his army of scholars to work to prove: (1) that his case was right, and (2) that the pope had no right to stop him. It was this tactic that came up trumps, for his scholars surpassed themselves. They reminded Henry that Joseph of Arimathea (perhaps even with Jesus) had planted the first church in England, at Glastonbury. This being the case, the church in England was older than that in Rome, founded by Peter. Thus (and here was the gravy) the church in England was independent of Rome; its headship belonging not to the pope, but the king.

And so, from 1532, a number of laws began to be passed to bring practices into line with this reality, the church in England being made increasingly independent from the pope, and increasingly dependent on the king. By 1533 these laws had made England independent enough for Henry to act. Coincidentally, at the same time he was able to arrange the appointment of a new Archbishop of Canterbury, Thomas Cranmer, who was happy to validate Henry's marriage to Anne, which had taken place secretly earlier in the year. Henry had what he wanted, and the following year (1534) the independence of the English church was complete as the Act of Supremacy proclaimed Henry 'supreme head of the church in England'.

Thomas Cranmer,
Archbishop of Canterbury

The speedy judgment meted out on those Catholics loyal to Rome who disputed this makes it easy to think that this was a Protestant Reformation in England, especially since the most famous victims (Thomas More, Henry's old Lord Chancellor, and John Fisher, Bishop of Rochester) were Luther's strongest opponents. However, while break with Rome it was, a Protestant Reformation it was not. Ever since Henry had written his *Defence of the Seven Sacraments*, he and Luther had kept up a bitter war of open letters with each other; and, sealing Henry's hatred of the Reformer, Luther then opposed Henry's dream of annulling his marriage. The king was never going to have much time for Lutheranism. Instead, the king made it quite clear that he would not be departing from any Catholic doctrine; he was only refusing to acknowledge the pope's supremacy in England.

However, having once used the Bible to argue the case for annulment against the pope, it was hard to resist the claim that the Bible was, after all, a higher authority than the pope. Also, those who had been prepared to help Henry break with Rome (and thus had now been rewarded with the highest offices) were often evangelical in their convictions, even if Henry was not. Thomas Cranmer, the new Archbishop of Canterbury, for instance, had had to be recalled from Germany to take up his post. It is a sign of his budding evangelicalism that when there, in Lutheran territory, he had got married, even though he was a priest. It is an even stronger sign that he kept his wife when recalled to England, where the marriage of priests was still illegal. (Of course, Mrs Cranmer needed to be kept hidden, and it was said that he had a large chest with air-holes specially made for her, so that when he travelled she could come along in her box. Some have seen her as a minor martyr of the Reformation for all those times when the box was packed upside down during the Archbishop's travels.) Another key evangel-ical figure was Henry's chief minister, Thomas Cromwell (not to be confused with Oliver Cromwell, the Lord Protector of England a century later). The king effectively gave him all the power over the church that the Pope had previously enjoyed (under Henry, of course). And then there was Anne Boleyn, an active sponsor of evangelicalism, who imported and distributed large quantities of evangelical literature, even introducing her husband to some of it. When she was queen, a number of the old guard of bishops died, and her command of the king's ear helped a number of evangelicals to be appointed in their place. Thus, while Henry's changes did not amount to a Protestant Reformation, an increasing number of well-placed evangelicals such as these were very happy to use them to evangelical ends.

The trouble was, as both evangelicals and Catholics found, the king's favour (and thus all influence) could be removed with terrifying suddenness. So it was for Anne Boleyn. Almost immediately she was pregnant, and thus enjoyed a unique honey-moon period in the king's goodwill. However, the child she bore was a girl (Elizabeth). The news could not have horrified Henry more. What had all his battles against pope and church been for? Upon hearing the news he is said to have galloped away from Greenwich and Anne down to Wiltshire, there to drown his sorrows with an old courtier, Sir John Seymour, who had an attractive daughter called Jane. The Seymour family were happy to fuel rumours about Anne, who, after miscarrying a boy, was fast falling from Henry's favour. It was whispered that she was having numerous affairs, was dabbling in witch-craft and even plotting to poison various members of the royal family. All absurd, but quite enough for Henry. Anne was arrested, found guilty of treason, and beheaded.

Anne Boleyn

The next day, Henry was betrothed to Jane Seymour, and ten days later, they were married. Like Anne, she only enjoyed Henry's goodwill for a short spell, but in her case because she died from complications in giving birth. Yet Henry remembered Jane as the only wife he ever really loved, essentially because she was the one who, after everything, bore him the much longed-for son and heir (Edward).

It had all added up to being an expensive few years for Henry, and his empty coffers were showing the strain. And so the prospect of all those monasteries (who, after all, were probably more loyal to Rome than the king) began to look increasingly irresistible to Henry. There were hundreds of them, the combined rents of their lands totting up to something really worth having. In any case, many were falling into ruins and only being sustained by gross irregularities. Thus, from 1536, egged on by his chief minister, Thomas Cromwell (who, of course, had his own

Protestant motives), Henry began the process of dissolving the monasteries.

All in all, it was quite a popular move. There was widespread irritation at the privileges of the clergy, and the wealthy were happy to buy up all those monastic lands being sold off at knock-down prices. And many of the monks and nuns seemed relieved, some now marrying each other, others content with their substantial pensions or becoming parish clergy. It may have been intended by Henry as little more than a royal smash-and-grab; the effect, however, was that, with church property now in their hands, the ruling classes were committed to Henry's reformation. There was no way back to old-style Roman Catholicism in England now. And (no doubt Cromwell's intention), closing down the monasteries effectively weed-killered the seedbed of much Catholicism.

At the same time, Henry was beginning to enjoy his role as the liberator of the English church as he rescued her from her captivity under the popes. 'Romish abuses' – the pilgrimages, relics and images that made money for the church – were slated for destruction, or worse: laughter. For instance, when Boxley Abbey in Kent was shut down, the revered Rood of Boxley (a crucifix which would jiggle excitedly whenever anyone made a generous donation) was uncovered as a fake, its miraculous movements attributable, not to God, but to levers, wires and a concealed monk. It was sent to London, where it was greeted with howls of laughter, sharp axes and a large bonfire.

While weed killer was being poured out on the old Catholicism, fertiliser began to be poured out on the thirsty young evangelical movement. In 1538, the king ordered that 'ye shall discourage no man from the reading or hearing of the Bible, but shall expressly provoke, stir and exhort every person to read the same as that which is the very lively word of God'. To that end, just two years after Tyndale had died crying 'Lord, open the King of England's eyes!', it was decreed that an English Bible be placed in every church. Traditionalist Catholics were, of course, shocked: what had been an offence to merit burning at the stake was suddenly commended behaviour. The Duke of Norfolk snorted 'I never read the Scripture, nor never will read it. It was merry in England afore the new learning came up; yea, I would all things were as hath been in time past.' Yet, on the whole, the law was received with red-hot enthusiasm. Six English Bibles were placed in St Paul's Cathedral, crowds immediately thronging round those who could read loud enough to make themselves heard. So great was the excitement that priests complained of how, even during the sermon, laypeople were reading the Bible aloud to each other. Private Bible-reading became a much more widespread feature of ordinary life, as even the illiterate learnt to read so as to gain immediate access to 'the very lively word of God'. And once that happened, it was very hard to go back: now butchers and bakers were discussing the Bible, coming to new convictions, and even daring to disagree with clergy over it. The church could no longer pontificate unchallenged. With Bible in hand, people were wanting to know where their priest got his ideas from.

However, Henry's reign was not a smooth and even shift from Catholicism to Protestantism. Henry could go through theological moods like he went through wives. After Jane Seymour's death, Cromwell tried to set Henry up with the Lutheran princess, Anne of Cleves. However, when Henry finally met her shortly before the marriage, he was so repulsed by 'the Flanders Mare', as he called her, that while the marriage had to go ahead, he would never consummate it. Instead, it was immediately annulled, and Cromwell paid for that fiasco with his head. The strongly Catholic Howard family then saw their moment, and introduced their brightest star, Catherine, to Henry. Henry did marry her, but it was a disaster, for Catherine was not content with a husband nearly thirty years older than herself. She was discovered having an affair, and with lightning speed followed Anne Boleyn to the execution block in the Tower of London. From Lutheran Anne, through Catholic Catherine, Henry turned at last to the reform-minded Catherine Parr, who, when Henry

The many wives of Windsor:

1509–33	Catherine of Aragon (marriage annulled)	Gave birth to Mary I
1533–6	Anne Boleyn (executed)	Gave birth to Elizabeth I
1536–7	Jane Seymour (died)	Gave birth to Edward VI
1540	Anne of Cleves (marriage annulled)	
1540–2	Catherine Howard (executed)	
1543–7	Catherine Parr (outlived Henry)	

died, must have been one of those wives relieved to outlive her husband.

In similar style, Henry legislated both for and against Catholicism, and both for and against Protestantism. A large anti-Protestant uprising in the North, though savagely put down by Henry, was an alarm-call to him that antagonizing the old order could be dangerous. He responded by announcing harsh measures against those who denied such traditional beliefs as transubstantiation and celibacy for priests (no doubt making Mr and Mrs Cranmer nervous). Disorderly popular Bible-reading led him, in 1543, to ban all unauthorized public exposition of the Bible, as well as all private reading of the Bible among the uneducated. Three years later all unauthorized translations of the Bible into English were also outlawed.

The events of 30 July 1540 make clear Henry's otherwise confusing religious views. On that day, six men were executed: three Catholics were hanged for the treason of denying Henry's supremacy over the church in England, and three evangelicals were burned for heresy. It was a brutal demonstration of what Henry wanted. He did not want England to become Protestant, but nor did he want England to be *Roman* Catholic. He wanted an *English* Catholicism, stripped of all Roman ties and Roman corruptions. The difficulty was, what was Roman (and so to be binned), and what was Catholic (and so to be kept)? Henry experienced the tension personally: while he had begun closing down the chantries (where priests prayed for souls in purgatory), he also made provision in his will for prayers to be said for his own soul. Just in case. Henry's other problem was, having once allowed the Bible to critique the pope and church practice, and having allowed it to be read by ordinary people, even for a few short years, it was almost impossible to stop where he had stopped. Completely unintentionally, Henry had unleashed a whirlwind, and it could be restrained for only so long.

England's King Josiah

A little unwisely, Henry had left the education of Prince Edward and Princess Elizabeth to Catherine Parr, and the finest tutors that could be found for them happened to be rather evangelical. Taught by the best, both grew up to be personally adamant evangelicals. Thus when, in 1547, Henry died and his son became King Edward VI, England was poised for a true reformation. Cranmer was thrilled: at last he would be able to take his wife out of her box and set about promoting unadulterated evangelicalism.

Edward was only nine when he became king, and thus his uncle, Edward Seymour, Duke of Somerset, ruled in his name as Lord Protector. It was he, who, with Cranmer, set about the work of Protestant reform. (Edward was no dupe in all this, however. Despite his youth, he had a loathing of what he contemptuously called 'papistry', as well as remarkably thought-through evangelical convictions.) For the first couple of years, Seymour and Cranmer worked gently, so as to acclimatize England to Protestantism slowly, rather than unnecessarily raise hackles.

Nevertheless, a lot changed: Henry's laws against evangelical beliefs and practices were overturned, allowing clergy to marry and people to receive both bread and wine in communion. Chantries were dissolved because they were based on the notion of purgatory, a belief that leads people away from trust in 'their very true and perfect salvation through the death of Jesus Christ'. Orders went out for images of saints to be removed from churches, and for altars (places for Christ to be re-sacrificed in the Mass) to be replaced with tables (places for a family meal). A prayer book in English (the *Book of Common Prayer*) was written to ensure that every church service was English in language and evangelical in content. Preaching was commanded in English, and many notable preachers, such as Hugh Latimer, started to become household names. For those clergy less capable of preparing their own sermons, a new book of homilies (off-the-rack sermons that could simply be read out) was produced, clearly explaining justification by faith alone. And for those getting ordained, there was a new expectation: now it was clear that

Hugh Latimer preaching to Edward VI, an avid lover of sermons

becoming a minister was not about being a priest who offers sacrifices (in the Mass), but primarily about preaching. To that end, those being ordained, instead of being invested with priestly clothes, were given a Bible.

It was all too much for some, and in 1549 there was a popular uprising in the south-west, mainly against the fact that the prayer book was in English (it made Cranmer despair that the rebels so passionately wanted a service in Latin, which they could not understand). Yet in that year John Dudley took over from Edward Seymour, and applied his foot more firmly to the accelerator of the Reformation. At the same time, England was becoming a refuge for continental reformers fleeing from the all-victorious armies of the Holy Roman Emperor. Martin Bucer of Strasbourg became Regius Professor of Divinity at Cambridge in time to help Cranmer write his prayer book. Peter Martyr Vermigli became Regius Professor of Divinity at Oxford in time to help him rewrite it.

Cranmer's two prayer books (1549 and 1552) are a good window on the passage of the Reformation in England. The 1549 version may have been written deliberately as stop-gap, digestible Reformation theology, preparing stomachs for the strong meat to come. In any case, while there was nothing about transubstantiation and the sacrifice of the Mass, other than its English it was not too grating for Catholic ears. On receiving the bread one would hear 'The Body of our Lord Jesus Christ, which was given for thee, preserve thy body and soul unto everlasting life'. It was thoroughly Lutheran, but a Catholic could eat with a happy conscience.

However, there were no Lutherans among all the refugee-theologians who came to England (something still felt today in the almost total lack of Lutheran flavour to English evangelicalism, which has always been much more Zwinglian and Calvinist). And, when Vermigli and others arrived, they hated the Lutheranism of the 1549 prayer book, and longed to make it more Swiss in feel. It worked. Whether Cranmer had been planning it in any case, or whether his own theology had changed, the words uttered at the giving of the bread in the 1552 version were 'Take and eat this in remembrance that Christ died for thee [which sounds Zwinglian], and feed on him in thy heart by faith with thanksgiving [which sounds Calvinist]'. No Catholic could be happy with that. The Reformation in England had moved on.

Then the runaway train of evangelical reform came to a bone-crunching halt with Edward's death, aged 15, in 1553. Fearing it coming, and knowing that it would be his arch-Catholic half-sister Mary who would come to the throne and undo all he had achieved, Edward had helped hatch a desperate plan. Dudley would make sure Lady Jane Grey, a resolutely evangelical cousin of Mary's and next in line to the throne after Henry's children, was installed as queen before Mary could be. And so, the moment Edward died, Jane was proclaimed Queen in London. All to no avail: Mary swiftly mustered support and entered London, sending Jane to the Tower. The plan had not accounted for the fact that most people cared more for a legitimate monarch than a Protestant one. Even Protestants had supported Mary, blissfully unaware of how severe she would be in dealing with them.

Bloody Mary: a repellent cocktail

Mary, however, was the daughter of Catherine of Aragon. Brought up the unquestioned princess of Henry's Roman Catholic court, she had suddenly been declared illegitimate and pressed to abandon her religion when Henry got rid of Catherine and broke with Rome. For Mary, Protestantism was not just a heresy, it was the reason for all her woes.

As quickly as she could, Mary returned England to Rome. Evangelical bishops were removed from office, Thomas Cranmer was replaced as Archbishop of Canterbury by Cardinal Pole, Bibles were removed from churches, married clergy were separated from their wives: quite simply, the national clock was set back to the time before all her father's changes. It was to be as if the whole distasteful affair had never happened. And in many ways, England seemed quite willing. There were, of course, a few riots against the new order, but there were also many who seemed relieved. All sorts of Catholic church furniture (images, priestly vestments, etc.) now reappeared, having been hidden by Catholics from Edward's purges. Clearly, Edward's reforms had not been popular with all.

That said, it was impossible to wipe out twenty years of history. Things could not go back to being quite how they had been. For one thing, all those monasteries and monastic estates could not be reclaimed, for while the new landowners might be happy to go to Mass, they were not so willing to hand back their land. And, it was simply too late now to act as if nobody had ever read a Bible or heard a sermon in English. People had begun to have doubts about traditional teaching, so that, even if they were not convinced evangelicals, they were not going to spend money on pilgrimages and practices that might not work. Even if the doubts had not come from Bible-reading, it was hard to venerate images after seeing the great Rood of Boxley ridiculed.

Mary's great problem was that all would be in vain if she did not produce an heir. She needed a baby. She needed a husband. But who could it be? She picked the future Philip II of Spain. It was not really a wise choice: Philip was an implacable enemy of Protestantism, and while people were prepared to tolerate a measure of Mary's Catholic clamp-down, grisly stories of the Spanish Inquisition made them much more concerned.

As it happened, their worst fears were realized. Seeing where the wind was blowing, many Protestants had sought refuge abroad in places like Calvin's Geneva; others decided to stay and operate quietly, secretly distributing their 'naughty books' and meeting in (often quite large) underground congregations. Those who stayed and did not lie low were burned. In all, and in stark contrast to the tolerance of Edward's reign, Mary's reign saw some 300 evangelicals burned for their faith, not counting the

The Oxford martyrs

Among Mary's most famous victims were the old Archbishop of Canterbury, Thomas Cranmer; the famous preacher and Bishop of Worcester, Hugh Latimer; and the Bishop of London, Nicholas Ridley. In 1555, Ridley and Latimer were burned together, back to back, at the end of Broad Street in Oxford. Latimer, aged about eighty, was the first to die, shouting through the flames: 'Be of good comfort, Master Ridley, and play the man; we shall this day light such a candle, by God's grace, in England, as I trust shall never be put out.' Unfortunately for Ridley the wood had been badly laid around him so that he suffered terribly, his legs burning off before the rest of him was touched. The horrible sight apparently moved hundreds to tears.

Five months later Thomas Cranmer was burned on the same spot. The old archbishop and architect of so much of the English Reformation, now nearly seventy, had, under extreme duress, renounced his Protestantism. It was a triumph for Mary's reign. Despite his recantation, however, he was such an embodiment of the Reformation that it was decided he should be burned in any case. It was a decision that would more than undo Mary's victory, for when the day came, Cranmer refused to read out his recantation. Instead he stated boldly that he was indeed a Protestant, though a cowardly one for forsaking his principles. In consequence, he announced, 'for as much as my hand offended, writing contrary to my heart, my hand shall first be punished there-for'. He was true to his word: as the fires were lit, he held out the hand that had signed his recantation so that it might burn first. Having briefly denied his Protestantism, Cranmer thus burned with movingly defiant bravery, and so died the first Protestant Archbishop of Canterbury.

The burning of Thomas Cranmer

many others who died in the horrendous conditions of sixteenth-century prisons. After Auschwitz, a few hundred may not sound like much, but for the day it was a true and terrifying holocaust.

The unexpected, steadfast courage of so many martyrs, coupled with the brutality of Mary's regime, could not fail to move the populace. The burnings seared into the national conscience an association of tyranny with Rome, while Mary's relations with Spain made the martyrs look like English patriots. Realizing this, in 1558 the decision was made to burn heretics away from the public eye, but by then it was too late.

Had Mary produced children, England would likely have remained officially Catholic. However, what Mary thought was the longed-for pregnancy turned out to be stomach cancer, and on 17 November 1558 she died, followed within hours by her Archbishop of Canterbury, Reginald Pole. In the end, 'Bloody' Mary's cocktail of burnings, Spanish connections and Rome had simply repelled the English from the Catholicism she sought to re-impose. And, watching it all from abroad, those in exile were more passionate than ever to return and purify England from such things. When Mary died, a tide of now white-hot anti-Catholic Protestantism would return to hit the English shore.

'This is the Lord's doing, and it is marvellous in our eyes'

It was with this verse, Psalm 118:23, that the young Princess Elizabeth apparently greeted the news that Mary had died and that she was now queen. No wonder she was relieved: almost miraculously, she had survived the holocaust, and the country could be reclaimed for Protestantism.

Henry's younger daughter Elizabeth was very much a chip off the old block. Imperious and relentlessly energetic, she had a quicksilver mind capable of lightning-fast repartee, and enough political cunning to survive Mary's reign without slipping up. And, being who she was, everyone knew she would reintroduce Protestantism. Her mother was Anne Boleyn, the cause of Henry's split with Rome, and since Rome refused to recognize Henry's marriage to Anne, Rome saw Elizabeth as illegitimate, meaning she couldn't be queen. Elizabeth had no choice but to be Protestant. However, it so happened that she was in fact a Protestant by personal and deeply-held conviction.

Within a year of becoming queen, Mary's religious reforms were undone, and a new Act of Supremacy proclaimed Elizabeth to be the 'supreme governor' of the Church of England (Henry had been 'supreme *head*', but this new title was intended to be less irritating both to Catholic ears and to those Protestants who did not believe a woman ever could be 'head'). Once more, the monarch, and not the pope, was in control.

On top of this, a new prayer book was provided, and again, its distinctive theology showed where things were at. Basically, the 1559 prayer book was very much like Cranmer's second, 1552 version, only toned down a bit. There was now no prayer for deliverance from the pope, his 'tyranny' and 'all his detestable enormities', for example. Once again, it was the words uttered at the giving of the bread that said so much. In the 1559 version they became, 'The Body of our Lord Jesus Christ, which was given for thee, preserve thy body and soul unto everlasting life [from the 1549 edition]. Take and eat this in remembrance that Christ died for thee, and feed on him in thy heart by faith with thanksgiving [from the 1552 edition].' In other words, the new prayer book was a compromise between Lutheranism and Swiss Protestantism.

This was to be exactly the sort of Protestantism Elizabeth would legislate. It was daringly and unmistakeably Protestant (the word 'compromise' does not imply that there was anything half-Catholic about it), but it was neither one brand of Protestantism nor the other. If Henry had established a very English (as opposed to Roman) Catholicism, Elizabeth established a very English (as opposed to especially Lutheran or Calvinist) Protestantism. Under Elizabeth, England was to be a united, Protestant nation. And that meant everyone had to go to church, where everyone would be presented with the same non-specific Protestantism. They didn't even have to agree with it. Catholics, for instance, did not have to take communion; they could privately believe whatever they wanted. They just had to conform and go along to church (or pay a very hefty fine each time they failed to show). As one of her contemporaries put it, she did not care to 'make windows into men's souls', only to unite the nation under herself and her faith.

It would be a mistake, however, to think of Elizabeth merely as a shrewd politician with little interest in theology. She was, personally, a convinced Protestant, reading the New Testament in Greek every day, as well as reading regularly from an English Bible and praying in English. When she had only just become queen, a bishop made the mistake of raising the bread (in the Catholic style, so that it might be worshipped) in her private chapel. Elizabeth stormed out and forbade any repeat of such behaviour at her coronation. At the opening of her first parliament, she ordered a Protestant to preach, and secretly (for fear of war) she provided aid to Protestants abroad.

Knowing her personal beliefs, the reformers happily shared sly winks with each other as this moderate Protestantism was rolled out onto the statue books. Surely this was just the beginning, the old tactic of stepping out slowly along the road of Reformation. It came as an extraordinary shock when it became

Contemporary sketch of Elizabeth I, by Nicholas Hilliard

clear that she saw it as her final word on the matter. As for those who came back from Geneva with advanced ideas of how the church could be further reformed, Elizabeth had little time for them. For while she was adamant that England be Protestant, she was equally adamant that this was no time for Protestant idealism. If England became too extreme, she feared, it would push anti-Protestant fervour on the Continent past boiling point, and thus threaten the safety of her realm. Spain or France might invade.

For a while everyone watched and waited. Elizabeth, after all, was a woman: if she married, that might change things; if she didn't, her lack of an heir would also change things. But after a decade it became clear that she was not going to marry, and she was not going to change. And so, in 1570, the pope tried to move things along by excommunicating her, officially depriving her of her throne, and calling on English Catholics to refuse to obey her. It was a bad move. Before, Catholicism had been tolerated; now it was treason. Since no Roman Catholic priests were being trained in England any more, the only spiritual supply-line for English Catholics was a trickle of priests, trained abroad, who came into the country to serve them privately. But now such priests, slipping across the border, were seen as dangerous agents of a hostile foreign power. After all, if they were loyal to the pope, they must be fomenting treason. And so Catholicism became a clandestine affair, with wealthy Catholic families hiding their priests in the priest-holes of their secluded country houses and pretending to conform.

Such secretive behaviour always multiplies suspicions, and over the years a national fear of 'the Catholic under the bed' grew. And it was not just paranoia. Not just the pope, but all the forces of the Catholic Counter-Reformation were set against the one united Protestant country in Europe. If Elizabeth's Protestant regime could be brought down, then Protestantism would be dealt a death blow.

The obvious move was to assassinate her, for if Elizabeth died, her loyally Catholic cousin, Mary Queen of Scots, was next in line and would take her place. Mary thus became the epicentre of Catholic plots against Elizabeth. They could hardly have had a figurehead less capable: where Elizabeth was shrewdness personified, Mary was anything but. Mary had already so successfully alienated everyone in Scotland that she had been forced to take refuge in England. To her mind this would not be a problem: surely her cousin Elizabeth would look after her. But Elizabeth was not particularly thrilled at the idea of having the mascot for all the assassination plots actually staying with her. She had Mary discreetly tucked away in the country under house arrest. And now the tables turned. Protestants on Elizabeth's council saw that, with Mary's son James being raised in safe Calvinist hands back in Scotland, Mary was a problem to be eliminated. If she died before Elizabeth, the crown would pass to Protestant James, and all would be well. Then one of Elizabeth's agents actually found hard evidence that Mary, embittered by her arrest, was part of a plot against Elizabeth. The game was up, and in 1587 Mary was executed.

The Protestant future of the crown was safe. However, the country was not, for the following year, 'Bloody' Mary's old husband, Philip II of Spain, attempted a full-scale armed invasion of England that the pope happily blessed as a crusade. If the nation was not united already, Philip's massive naval armada sailing up the English Channel did it. With the help of some ferocious storms, the armada was defeated. It was clear to all in England: God had saved his true people (Protestant) and judged the wicked (Catholic). A medal was struck to commemorate the victory, bearing an inscription that echoed Exodus 15:10 and Israel's salvation from the Egyptian army: *Afflavit Deus et dissipantur* ('God blew and they were scattered'). Clearly, God had smiled on Elizabeth's Protestantism. And, just as clearly to Elizabeth's mind, that meant God did not think she needed to go further down the road of reform, as some of her subjects thought.

By the end of her reign, in 1603, there was no doubt: to be English was to be Protestant. To be Catholic was to be a treacherous tool of foreign powers. The cult of the Virgin Mary had been replaced by the cult of the virgin queen, Elizabeth. How things had changed! Back in 1560, the Calvinist Geneva Bible had been produced, full of explanatory notes, so that when, for example, the reader came across a difficult word like 'antichrist', a note would explain 'that is, the Pope with the whole bodie of his filthie creatures'. At the time, that was a view held only by the hard-core. But by the end of Elizabeth's reign, that the pope was the antichrist was obvious to everyone.

As much as anything, Elizabeth's long reign (1558–1603) turned out to be a war of attrition against Catholicism. When she first came to the throne, nobody expected it. But as the years passed, Catholic practices simply fell into disuse, and Catholic priests trained in the old ways died out. In their place, Cranmer's liturgy and homilies were heard by all, week after week; soon the only theology pastors could access was Protestant; soon the only Bible people knew was English, and ownership and knowledge of it slowly filtered into even the most rural areas. Elizabeth's long reign ensured that the nation was Protestant. What it could never do was ensure that the people were themselves evangelical.

North of the border

Things always work differently in Scotland, though the Scottish Reformation started out along familiar lines. At the same time as Lutheran literature was being smuggled into England and discussed in Cambridge, it was making inroads into Scotland, finding eager readers in St Andrews. And, just as in England, some of the evangelical converts began to preach the new doctrines. However, none of this made much difference until, in 1528, one of them, Patrick Hamilton, was arrested and burned for heresy in St Andrews. It raised the profile of evangelicalism in Scotland, making many wonder what the new teaching was, why it was so dangerous, and why a man would die for it.

One thing that was different in Scotland was that the king (James V, at the time) was already in almost complete control of the church in his country. And so, to his mind, there was no need to break with Rome as Henry VIII of England had done. What would he gain? The Scottish crown was simply never going to be interested in cutting loose from Rome.

Then, in 1542, James died, opening a window of opportunity for the Reformation. The rightful monarch was now the infant Mary, Queen of Scots, but ruling as her regent was James Hamilton, the Earl of Arran. The next year saw something extraordinary: 'Arran's godly fit'. Arran himself had an extraordinary ability to flip-flop between Catholicism and Protestantism, but that year he was Protestant. And the result was a year of pro-Protestant legislation: a Bible in the vernacular was sanctioned (and sold well); evangelical preachers were commissioned; the leading Roman Catholic, Cardinal David Beaton of St Andrews, was even arrested.

Then Beaton spearheaded a backlash, and, a year having passed, Arran decided to be a Catholic again. Reading a vernacular Bible was declared illegal again, and, as a clear sign to all that the good old days were back, the leading evangelical preacher, George Wishart, was captured, tried, and burned as a heretic.

However, Scottish Protestants were not the sort to take such treatment lying down. A small, disguised gang broke into St Andrews castle, murdered Beaton, hung his body from his window and proceeded to take the castle over. For the next year the castle became a place of retreat for Scottish Protestants, who held it until bombed into submission by French troops called in to help.

Most of the defeated defendants were condemned to be galley-slaves aboard French ships, chained to benches to row throughout the day under the threat of a whip. Among them was

John Knox

Wishart's old broadsword-wielding bodyguard and later preacher to the castle defend-ants, John Knox. His fellow prisoners already knew his theology: his first sermon, on the pope as the whore of Babylon, had made that clear. But now, on his ship, they began to know his mettle. They used to be threatened with torture if they did not show reverence to the Mass when it was celebrated onboard, or to an image of the Virgin Mary. However, when Knox refused and the image of Mary was forced in his face for him to kiss, Knox grabbed it and threw it overboard. After that, their captors stopped trying, and after nearly two years of making their lives a misery, he was released.

Knox spent a while in England, trying to push Cranmer to speed up his Reformation, but when 'Bloody' Mary came to the throne, he left for Geneva. For Knox, Geneva was paradise: 'the most perfect school of Christ that ever was in the earth since the days of the apostles', he called it. It got him dreaming of what his native Scotland could be like. He did get to travel over the next few years, even managing to slip back into Scotland briefly, where he was warmly received by growing numbers of Scottish Protestants, who were beginning to see him as something of a leader-in-exile. But for the most part, he waited in Geneva, watching with mounting fury as he saw events in Britain unfold.

In 1558 his anger boiled over and he unleashed from his pen *The First Blast of the Trumpet Against the Monstrous Regiment of Women*. By the 'regiment' (rule) of women, he was referring to the reigns of the two Catholic queens, Mary, Queen of Scots, and 'Bloody' Mary of England. To Knox's mind, the root of all the horrors being unleashed in Britain was the 'monstrous' fact that women were ruling, when rulership was the preserve of men. It was disastrously timed, for shortly after publication, 'Bloody' Mary died, which should have left Knox free to return to England. However, there was no way Elizabeth was going to have the author of the *Trumpet Blast* in her realm. It may not have been written with her in mind at all, but Elizabeth never forgave Knox for the insult, and always harboured a deep suspicion of anything from Geneva thereafter.

The next year (1559), however, Knox finally got to return to Scotland. Immediately, his volcanic sermons stoked Protestant feeling (and a few riots). He was declared an outlaw, but very quickly a powerful band of Protestant nobles and people were prepared to defend Knox and fight for their Protestantism. At the same time, just as in England, Catholicism was starting to be associated with being foreign. Mary, Queen of Scots, was herself all too French: brought up in France, still living in France, married to a Frenchman, with a French mother (who had taken over from Arran as Mary's regent); for many Scots, it felt uncomfortably like Scotland was being turned into a province of France. And so Scottish patriotism started to fuse with Scottish Protestantism in a bid to be rid of the Catholic French.

Of course, all this was music to Elizabeth's ears, down in England. She loved the idea of having a Protestant Scotland to her north, instead of being trapped in what was otherwise an uncomfortable Catholic vice, with a Catholic Scotland to her north and Catholic France to her south. She decided to send troops north to help the Protestants win the day. Their very appearance was enough to swing things, and in 1560 the Scottish Parliament was able to decree that the pope no longer had any authority in Scotland, and instead that all doctrine and practice had to conform to a new confession of faith (the Scots Confession) drawn up by John Knox. Mary, Queen of Scots, might not have liked it, but she was still in France, and when she arrived in Scotland a year later, she would have to accept it. Scotland was now a Calvinist country.

It was an extraordinary turnaround. In 1558, both England and Scotland had been Catholic; in 1560, they were Protestant. Of course, as in England, it would take more time for Protestantism to become a popular, personal conviction. At Easter in 1561, for example, less than one in ten of the population of Edinburgh were prepared to receive a Calvinist Lord's Supper. It was not that they were especially attached to the Mass; it was that they had yet to understand the new theology. They needed trained preachers and a Protestant liturgy before they could ever take evangelicalism to their hearts.

Politics and theology

What is perhaps most telling about the reformations in England and Scotland is how very different they were, both from each other, and from the reformations in Wittenberg, Zurich and Geneva. Simply put, a reformation driven more by theology looks quite unlike a reformation driven more by politics. For the kings and queens of England, politics was central to their thinking in a way that just was not the case for Luther, Zwingli and Calvin. The same can be seen in the difference between the reformations in England and Scotland: in England, the Reformation was very much a top-down affair, driven by the monarchs (and used by reformers); in Scotland, it was more bottom-up, demanded by the people despite the monarch.

If anything, what that difference proves is how the Reformation, at its heart, was about doctrine. It was not a quest for political, social or moral reform dressed up in theological clothes; deeper down than anything else was a set of theological questions: 'What is the gospel?' 'How can we know?' 'What is salvation, and how can I be saved?' 'Who are God's people, and what is the church?' The very fact that it is so easy to spot the difference between Martin Luther and Henry VIII says it all. It was quite possible to use the Reformation for political ends (as Henry did), but the Reformation itself was a theological revolution (as Luther showed).

Notes

1 R. Bainton, *Erasmus of Christendom* (William Collins Sons & Co., 1969), p. 153.

6 Reforming the Reformation: the Puritans

Who were the Puritans?

'Puritan': the word has always been more a weapon than a description. For the vast majority it is verbal mud that, once hurled, makes the victim look a laughable, po-faced, lemon-sucking prig. For the small minority it is brandished as a description of a united golden team with the most impeccable theological and spiritual credentials.

The word was coined as a term of abuse shortly after Elizabeth became queen: for the average Englishman, there was the Catholic 'papist' on one side, and the 'precisionist' or 'puritan', who went too far the other way. It suggested a nit-picking, holier-than-thou sort, who considered themselves purer than the rest. It was certainly not a fair description: those it was applied to clearly never thought of themselves as pure (far, far from it, as their constant testimony to their own sinfulness demonstrates). But neither was it a very precise description: recognized Puritans differed from one another, often sharply. They could disagree over what the cross was about; they could disagree over how, exactly, to be saved; the poet John Milton, an undoubted Puritan, did not even believe in the Trinity, the God of all Christian creeds.

Who, then, were the Puritans? Perhaps John Milton put it best, when he spoke of 'the reforming of the Reformation', for that was the united goal of all Puritans. It was not that they thought they were pure, it was that they wanted to purify what in the church and in themselves had not yet been purified. They wanted reform, and while they had some different ideas as to what that should look like, they wanted to apply the Reformation to everything it had not yet touched. They thought the Reformation was a good thing, but that it was not yet complete.

Right but repulsive?

Before seeing their story, some of the mud that has been thrown at them needs to be wiped off if we are ever to understand them.

For one thing, they did not even look like what we think of as the stereotypical Puritan. We imagine that, amidst all the gaudy puffed sleeves and bodices of the Elizabethan period, and the jolly ruffs and doublets of the laughing Cavaliers, the Puritans just wore black – and scowled. That is how their portraits show them, for that was their Sunday best (and sitting for portraits was a formal thing). But on other days they might wear all the colours of the rainbow. John Owen, probably the greatest Puritan theologian, would walk through Oxford 'hair powdered, cambric band with large costly band strings, velvet jacket, breeches set round at knees with ribbons pointed, and Spanish leather boots with cambric tops'.

Nor were they a crowd of inveterate sourpusses.

Contrary to popular impression, the Puritan was no ascetic. If he continually warned against the vanity of the creatures as misused by fallen man, he never praised hair shirts or dry crusts. He liked good food, good drink and homely comforts; and while he laughed at mosquitoes, he found it a real hardship to drink water when the beer ran out.[1]

Bluntly, any attempt to say what 'all Puritans' were like is going to be misleading, given what a large, and often diverse, group they were. So, of course, some were quite dour: William Prynne, for instance, could write that 'Christ Jesus our pattern . . . was always mourning, never laughing'. But what might be true of one is by no means necessarily true of another.

What can be said of many of them, though, is that their zeal for reforming all of life could lead to a certain amount of pedantry. The later American Puritan Cotton Mather, for instance, once wrote in his diary:

> I was once emptying the cistern of nature, and making water at the wall. At the same time, there came a dog, who did so too, before me . . . [Shocked that his action was debasing him 'into the condition of the beast'] I resolved that it should be my ordinary practice, whenever I stop to answer the one or other necessity of nature to make it an opportunity of shaping in my mind some holy, noble, divine thought.

A little too serious, one might think! But again, we cannot assume that all Puritans did the same.

The most important trait that leaves the Puritans so misunderstood is the one that really did unite them all: their passionate love for the Bible, for Bible study, and for listening to sermons. Again and again we hear of Puritans happily travelling hours to hear a good, long sermon, and of how they thought a good Bible study better than an evening's dancing. Sermons up to seven hours long were not unheard-of. Laurence Chaderton, the extraordinarily long-lived Master of that nursery of Puritanism, Emmanuel College, Cambridge, once apologized to his congregation for preaching to them for two straight hours. Their response was to cry 'For God's sake, Sir, go on, go on!' To people who have never experienced the Bible as something thrilling, such behaviour sounds at best boring, and at worst deranged. But Europe had been without a Bible people could read for something like a thousand years. To be able to read God's words, and to see in them such good news that God saves sinners, not on the basis of how well they repent, but entirely by his own grace, was like a burst of Mediterranean sunshine into the grey world of religious guilt. It was almost intoxicatingly attractive and alluring.

A parliament of English puritans: Thomas Gouge, William Bridge, Thomas Manton, John Flavel, Richard Sibbes, Stephen Charnock, William Bates, John Owen, John Howe, Richard Baxter

Really, to fail to understand that makes it impossible to understand the Puritans. Take, for example, an account of a typically Puritan event: 'Roaring' John Rogers preaching a sermon in the pretty little village of Dedham on the Suffolk-Essex border. Here John Howe records Thomas Goodwin's memory:

And in that sermon he [Rogers] falls into an expostulation with the people about their neglect of the Bible (I am afraid it is more neglected in our days); he personates God to the people, telling them, 'Well, I have trusted you so long with my Bible; you have slighted it, it lies in such and such houses all covered with dust and cobwebs; you care not to look into it. Do you use my Bible so? Well, you shall have my Bible no longer.' And he takes up the Bible from his cushion, and seemed as if he were going away with it, and carrying it from them; but immediately turns again and personates the people to God, falls down on his knees, cries and pleads most earnestly, 'Lord, whatsoever thou dost to us, take not thy Bible from us; kill our children, burn our houses, destroy our goods; only spare us thy Bible, only take not away thy Bible.' And then he personates God again to the people: 'Say you so? Well, I will try you a little longer; and here is my Bible for you, I will see how you will use it, whether you will love it more, whether you will value it more, whether you will observe it more, whether you will practice it more, and live more according to it.' But by these actions . . . he put all the congregation into so strange a posture that he never saw any congregation in his life. The place was a mere Bochim, the people generally (as it were) deluged with their own tears; and he told me that he himself when he got out, and was to take horse again to be gone, was fain to hang a quarter of an hour upon the neck of his horse weeping, before he had power to mount, so strange an impression was there upon him, and generally upon the people, upon having been thus expostulated with for the neglect of the Bible.

The whole story is quite incomprehensible without appreciating that, for the Puritan, the Bible was the most valuable thing that this world affords. Puritanism was about reforming all of life under the sole authority of the Bible. It was something that would put the fear of God into the authorities.

Weeding out 'popery'

Puritanism began when Elizabeth established the Church of England with her own peculiarly English Protestantism. All Protestants were delighted to see England recovered from Rome, but those who would soon be called Puritans were those who could never settle for what Elizabeth had created. Not that they wished to leave the Church of England; it was still the church, after all (the few who did leave in the early years of Elizabeth's reign are not generally known as Puritans). But in their view it was a church too wishy-washy by half, in need of a good deal more reforming. Many of them had seen how things could be while in exile from Mary in Switzerland, and much as today the English shake their heads when they compare their train system to the Swiss one, so the Puritans shook theirs when they compared Elizabeth's Church of England with Calvin's Geneva. For example, Church of England ministers were still called priests and wore priestly vestments: surely, thought the Puritans, wouldn't that lead people to think that they were there, not primarily to teach, but to offer the sacrifice of the Mass? The sign of the cross was still used at baptism: surely that distracted people from the true meaning of baptism, turning it into a mere ritual? A wedding ring was still given at Church of England marriages: did that not encourage people to think of marriage as a sacrament, as Rome argued, with the ring as the external sign? People were still to kneel at communion (to receive, instead of real bread, a wafer, so that none of Christ's body might fall to the floor): did that not imply worshipping the bread and wine, as in the Mass? And what of such practices as confirmation? Where was that in the Bible?

The trouble was, while Elizabeth was a Protestant, she disliked what she called 'new-fangledness', and instinctively liked the old ways (like swearing, Catholic-style, 'By God's Body!'). The sort of things the Puritans squirmed at she thought were entirely inconsequential. In her mind, the matter of religion in England was settled in 1559: England was Protestant, and no more need be said. For the Puritans, on the other hand, the idea of a religious 'settlement' was entirely against a fundamental Protestant conviction, that the church must continually be reformed to bring it more into line with the word of God.

And it wasn't just how things looked on a Sunday. No Puritan could consider the work of reformation complete when the majority of the population still had little or no understanding of justification by faith alone. It was not enough to reform how the church operated; the Reformation was about transforming individual lives, achieving not just an external Protestantism, but an internal, heart-felt evangelicalism.

The seedbeds for it all were the universities, especially Cambridge, where influential dons such as Laurence Chaderton

---

Reforming souls

Though Richard Baxter ministered nearly a century after this first generation of Puritans, all Puritans would have heartily echoed what he said on this issue:

Alas! can we think that the reformation is wrought, when we cast out a few ceremonies, and changed some vestures, and gestures, and forms! Oh no, sirs! it is the converting and saving of souls that is our business. That is the chiefest part of reformation.

Richard Baxter (1615–91)

And Baxter was to be the Puritan model of what that entailed. In order to accomplish such reformation, he believed that regular preaching was not enough; he needed to spend time with individuals ensuring that they understood the gospel for themselves, applying it to their situation and personally tutoring them. And so, in his parish of Kidderminster in the 1650s, he set about seeing every parishioner once a year, spending about an hour with each family, and seeing about fifteen families a week. The result was staggering:

> In a word [never believe a Puritan when they say they'll be brief!], when I came thither first, there was about one Family in a Street that worshipped God and called on His Name, and when I came away there were some Streets where there was not past one Family in the side of a Street that did not so; and that did not by professing serious Godliness, give us hopes of their sincerity.

took the view that the main purpose of the university was to supply the land with preachers. Fellows at his college were not allowed to stay for long, because it was expected that they should head out to find themselves a pulpit. And when they did head out, the friendships they had formed at university were key for mutual support.

Partly because of those connections, Puritan preachers tended to know who the other Puritans in their vicinity were; and before long, a practice had grown up of gathering for what they called 'prophesyings'. At these, a few clergy would preach in turn, and then the sermons would be discussed, helping the preachers to preach better, and the people listening to benefit from a month's worth of sermons in a day. The prophesyings were wildly popular: people would travel for miles (in an age when travel was slow) to enjoy such a hefty serving of preaching, and the well-to-do often did all they could to help sponsor the events, by supplying the preachers with dinner and wine. And they were hugely significant: here were events where doctrine was discussed freely with reference to the Bible, rather than being handed down from on high.

One of the effects of such freedom of discussion was that, by the 1570s, a generation had grown up that was less tolerant of waiting for reform. They were willing to have stronger views. Many began arguing that real reformation required that every part of the way the church worked must have direct biblical warrant. It could get a little absurd: the minister must stand in one place during the service, it was argued, because Peter 'stood up in the midst of the disciples' (Acts 1:15, KJV); there must be two Sunday services because Numbers 28:9 speaks of two burnt offerings each Sabbath, and so on. Some also started wondering if this model of the prophesyings was how the church should be governed, with (instead of bishops) groups of clergy meeting to decide how all the churches in their area should work. In other words, they began to advocate Presbyterianism for the Church of England.

Such talk, of course, sounded like anarchism to Elizabeth and the establishment. When, in 1570, Thomas Cartwright, the recently appointed Professor of Divinity at Cambridge, ran a series of lectures arguing for Presbyterianism, he was swiftly removed from his professorship. Six years later, Elizabeth decided to put an end to the whole menace of the prophesyings, and ordered her new Archbishop of Canterbury, Edmund Grindal, to suppress them. A thoroughgoing evangelical, Grindal could not countenance muzzling the word of God, especially when so many were benefiting from it, and so he refused. Unsurprisingly, he was put under house arrest at Lambeth Palace, where he remained, deprived of any power to help the Puritans, until his death in 1583.

His successor, John Whitgift, was the dictatorial headmaster-type who liked the idea of everyone signing statements that they would be good boys and adhere to the *Book of Common Prayer*, rather than being awkward about those bits they didn't like. Many could not, and so were suspended from their ministries. It may have tidied things up for the archbishop, but it also pushed the Puritans into a deeper, united disgruntlement. In 1588 a backlash began with the publication of a series of tracts by 'Martin Marprelate' (a pseudonym that managed simultaneously to wink in Martin Luther's direction and make a less savoury gesture in the direction of the prelates [bishops]). The tracts were outrageous, accusing Whitgift of holding homosexual orgies in Lambeth Palace, referring to the other bishops as dunghills and servants of Satan, and so on. 'Martin' had clearly enjoyed writing them, but such mud-slinging was never going to be very productive. More than ever, Puritanism was now associated with sedition and anarchy.

The hunt for the secret press on which the tracts were produced was turned into an excuse to spy out dangerous nonconformity in any Puritan preacher's home. Within a few short years, a legal clampdown on Puritanism was in force, with the 1593 Parliamentary Act Against Puritans, the hanging of separatist leaders, and the placing of many major Puritan figures in dire peril. Now was the time for their enemies to kick them while they were down.

Among their most bitter foes were the playwrights. Puritans had a number of gripes with the theatres: not only did they in many ways function as the brothels of the day, but also, it was clear to the Puritans that male actors playing female roles (as they did, since there were no actresses) would encourage sodomy. Yet playwrights did not like to hear their masterpieces described as 'the very pomps of the Devil', and so now they fought back to make the Puritan a standard figure of fun in their works (think of the Puritan Malvolio in Shakespeare's *Twelfth Night*). And of course, such lampooning was eagerly lapped up by people who did not want to have their alehouse and theatre habits challenged by the Puritans.

They were dark days for the Puritans in the last decade of Elizabeth's reign. Some got through it by ignoring the politics and getting on with the real issue of reformation (the reforming of souls); others endured it in the knowledge that it could not be long before James VI of Scotland would be king of England.

The wisest fool in Christendom

Reared on a strict diet of haggis and Calvinism, James was the hope of every Puritan. Now at last, they thought, they would have a properly reformed monarch. And what is more, he was highly educated: the author of numerous treatises, from con-demnations of tobacco and witchcraft to works of politics and theology, he would surely appreciate the theological issues at stake. So, when Elizabeth died, before James even made it to London, he was presented with a petition from the Puritans, asking for a number of changes to be made to what they still saw as a slightly 'popish' prayer book.

In response, James called for a conference to be held at Hampton Court the following year, 1604, at which both Puritans and those happy with the prayer book could put their cases to him. Unfortunately for the Puritans, James was used to dealing with the fiery, take-no-prisoners style of John Knox's followers in Scotland, and when the time came, he took the respectful submissiveness of the English Puritan delegates to mean they had no serious grievance. Worse, James suspected that the Puritans were really angling for a Presbyterian church order, which, James said (in his thick Scottish burr) 'agreeth as well with the monarch as God and the Devil . . . Then Jack and Tom and Will and Dick shall meet and at their pleasure censor me.' And that, for James, was the nub of it: reform was all very well, but only so long as it did not involve any chipping-away at his divinely given authority as king. The Puritans came away with virtually nothing. The only significant Puritan idea that James did like was for a new version of the Bible to be prepared. James' mind raced: at last he could be rid of those awkward marginal notes in the Geneva Bible that advocated such worrying things as disobedi-ence to a bad king. And so King James' authorized version of the Bible was commissioned.

It was certainly not all doom and gloom for the Puritans. The next year (1605), the foiling of the Catholic Gunpowder Plot – a

The Gunpowder Plot conspirators

plot to kill the king and his government by blowing up the Houses of Parliament – tipped national opinion away from Catholicism and into their favour. James even began appointing some enthusiastically Puritan bishops, giving Puritanism an influential voice.

However, the fact that James demanded conformity as strongly as Elizabeth ever had was the final straw for some. They had endured Elizabeth's reign of compromise in hope that better times were ahead, but now that James was on the throne and singing the same tune, it was clear compromise was there to stay. If that was not bad enough, James sometimes seemed to go out of his way to antagonize the Puritans. In 1618, for example, he issued his *Book of Sports*, which declared that most sports that did not involve cruelty to animals were entirely acceptable ways to pass a Sunday afternoon. The cruelty to Puritans was, ministers were required to read this out from their pulpit. To most Puritans, who by this time were generally strict Sabbatarians, this was nothing less than a direct challenge. They either refused to read it out or would add at the end, 'Remember the sabbath day, to keep it holy'.

All this being the case, James' reign saw a growing number of Puritans leave, some just leaving the Church of England, some leaving England itself. In 1607 one congregation upped and sailed to Holland (a popular choice), but a bleak existence there made them look further afield. And so, in 1620, meeting up with some eager émigrés in Plymouth, they set sail for the new world aboard the *Mayflower*. It was a move that would catch the Puritan imagination: the godly fleeing oppression in England looked like Israel fleeing Egypt; and, just like Israel, they were seeking a promised land of freedom. There they would establish a New England and build a New Jerusalem. There they would create a fully reformed society, freed from the shackles of the old world; it would be 'a city on a hill', a beacon to the world. It was a vision so attractive that soon tens of thousands were following it.

However, in old England, Puritanism would never again be a united force, but was increasingly a collection of splinter-groups, divided over whether to stay in the Church of England, and over an increasing number of theological questions. And the more people left to enjoy a greater degree of their own idea of Christian purity, the more the Puritan influence was weakened. In horror at what was fast becoming a major Puritan problem, Richard Sibbes said 'What a joyful spectacle is this to Satan and his faction, to see those that are separated from the world fall in pieces among themselves! Our discord is our enemy's melody.'

Richard Sibbes vs. the danger of moralism
The whole story of the Reformation in Britain shows how easily Protestantism could become a mere political party. In England it was all too simple to be zealously anti-Catholic while having no understanding or experience of God's saving grace. When just about everybody went to church, it was entirely undemanding to be nominally Protestant. And, as much as anything else, it was this that the Puritans fought as they urged people to a personal reformation.

However, there was a considerable danger for such a fight (one that threatened not only Puritanism, but also its sister-movement in Germany, Lutheran Pietism). That is, the desire to have people respond to the gospel could lead to a focus on the response, not the gospel. So, in looking for reformed lives (the sign that a person had responded rightly to the gospel), it was easy to let a concern for growth in personal holiness eclipse the original Reformation focus on justification. In other words, the danger for the Puritans was that they would be tempted to concentrate on holy living in response to the gospel at the expense of proclaiming the free, saving grace of God.

Thus the experience of all too many church-goers was that they heard many a sermon on the Ten Commandments, but yet remained fuzzy on how or if God would ever forgive them. As a result they acted as though their salvation depended on their holiness of life (Luther's original problem). And, when coupled with strong warnings to avoid damnation (and these could be strong: William Perkins 'would pronounce the word *damn* with such emphasis, as left a doleful echo in his auditors' ears a long while after'), many were left extremely anxious. The result, said Thomas Goodwin, was that in their concern for their spiritual state, 'the minds of many are so wholly taken up with their own hearts, that . . . Christ "is scarce in all their thoughts".' Unable to look out and trust in Christ's free grace, they were forced to a morbid introspection, attempting to see if their own hearts felt good enough, or if there was any faith there that they could trust in (and so trusting, not Christ, but their own faith for their salvation).

It was here that some of the Puritan ministries that are still most refreshing came in with the cure. Richard Sibbes is a glowing example. Sibbes (1577–1635) was trained in Cambridge, became a preacher there at Holy

Trinity Church, and then in 1617 became preacher to the prestigious Gray's Inn, one of the London Inns of Court. He held this position until his death, and it served as an opportunity to address some of the most important

figures of the day, many of whom would govern England in the turbulent years to come. In 1626, Sibbes was also made master of Katharine Hall, Cambridge (and soon became the preacher at Holy Trinity again). Sibbes then simultaneously held three of the most influential posts in England, using them to advance the message of a gracious God's sweet gospel. It is as a preacher, however, that Sibbes is best remembered. Known by contemporaries as the 'honey-mouthed', the 'heavenly Dr Sibbes', the 'sweet dropper', he was the most effective evangelistic preacher of his day, so appealing that hardened sinners were said deliberately to avoid hearing him, for fear he would convert them.

Richard Sibbes

Speaking into the culture of introspection and moral self-reliance, Sibbes preached a series of sermons on Matthew 12:20 (itself a citation of Isaiah 42:3), 'A bruised reed shall he not break, and smoking flax shall he not quench, till he send forth judgment unto victory' (KJV). Aimed at 'the binding up of a broken heart', the sermons were published as *The Bruised Reed and the Smoking Flax*, and were instrumental in the conversion of at least one other major Puritan figure, Richard Baxter.

The verse Sibbes expounded refers, of course, to Jesus, and it is a striking feature of Sibbes's preaching how strongly Christ-focused he is. And that is no accident: Sibbes sought to draw his audience's eyes from their own hearts to the Saviour, for 'there are heights, and depths, and breadths of mercy in him above all the depths of our sin and misery'. How so? Because, since 'God's love resteth on Christ, as well pleased in him, we may gather that he is as well pleased with us, if we be in Christ!' Thus Christian confidence in our spiritual state rests not on our strength of faith or performance, but upon 'the joint agreement of all three persons of the Trinity', that the Father loves the Son, and it is in the Son's merits, and not our own, that Christians are loved. Because God is a loving community, Christians can be confident.

Then, instead of simply laying moral burdens on young and struggling Christians, Sibbes showed them Christ's attractiveness so that they might love him from the heart. From then, the Christian's first task is 'to warm ourselves at this fire of his love and mercy in giving himself for us'. Only when Christians do that do they truly stop sinning from the heart (whereas when they merely alter their behaviour it does nothing for the sin of the heart). In other words, Sibbes believed that the solution to sin is not the attempt to live without sin, but the gospel of God's free grace.

The Bruised Reed is a clarion call for ministers to minister more like Christ, not crushing the weak with burdens, but blowing the oxygen of the gospel onto the smouldering wick of sputtering Christian lives. Significantly, Sibbes ends *The Bruised Reed* with a reference to Luther (by whom, he says, God 'kindled that fire which all the world shall never be able to quench'). Sibbes seems to suggest that, even in reforming the

Reformation, the real spirit of reformation could be lost, and all the doubts and anxieties of medieval Catholicism come streaming back in through the back door of a zealous Christian moralism that had lost sight of the grace of God. It was to maintain this essence of the Reformation that Sibbes and Puritans like him sought to teach and proclaim 'the gracious nature and office of Christ; the right conceit of which is the spring of all service to Christ, and comfort from him'.

Pushed to breaking-point

Before he even became king, James I's stuttering son Charles faced an uphill public relations battle. In a naïve bid to reconcile Protestantism and Catholicism, his father had tried to marry him to the Catholic daughter of the King of Spain. People took it that he wished the Spanish Armada had succeeded. Charles had enough sense to pull out of that one, but the moment he became king in 1625 he made just as disastrous a decision, to marry the French princess, Henrietta Maria, instead. And when she arrived in Dover with a swarm of Catholic priests in tow, people could only conclude that Charles was a secret papist.

Certainly Charles was a high churchman, and stuffed the church with bishops more to his taste (the 'high church' party in the Church of England despised the Reformation – or 'Deformation', as they called it – deliberately building their new churches in a pre-Reformation style). He even managed to appoint his dream Archbishop of Canterbury, the diminutive William Laud, an Oxford academic who would never be trusted by the Cambridge Puritans. Laud was never a man much able to win people over; he seemed to reserve all displays of warmth for his pet cats and giant tortoise. The thing was, he didn't even seem to try. When Charles re-issued his father's *Book of Sports*, Laud merrily suspended all clergy who refused to play ball and read it from the pulpit. But it was Laud's love of liturgy and orderliness (*his* liturgy and orderliness) that really got people's backs up. For example, he installed communion rails in the churches; and that, people reckoned, was either the attempt of a cat-lover to curb the freedom of the average Englishman's beloved dog (people were quite used to bringing their dogs to church), or it was popish. Given that Laud insisted people kneel at the rail for communion, it looked like the latter. And then there was how different Laud's clergy were: one can see how much things had changed by the confusion of one old lady in Norwich, who, seeing her minister standing at the communion table in scarlet mass-vestments, wondered why the mayor was officiating.

All this was quite enough to provoke massive popular resistance and push many more into sympathy with the Puritans. But the air started getting hotter. In 1637, three tub-thumpers were arrested and brought before the Star Chamber, a court of law that seemed beyond the law. William Prynne had criticized the lifestyle of the queen, Henrietta Maria; Henry Burton had described all bishops as 'upstart mushrumps'; and John Bastwicke had also criticized Laud's bishops. For these crimes their ears were carved off, Prynne's face was branded, and they were dragged through the streets of London to the stocks, where it was expected, as was custom, for the mob to pelt them with garbage. Instead, the crowd showed their support for the men. It was ominous, and yet it was not surprising: this was a generation reared on stories of the martyrdoms under 'Bloody' Mary, all faithfully recorded by John Foxe in his *Book of Martyrs*, a work that had long been on display in every cathedral and many churches. The fates of Prynne, Burton and Bastwicke just looked too uncomfortably similar.

Despite the murmurings, Charles and Laud pressed on. That same year, 1637, Charles decided it was high time for his realm of Scotland to be brought into line with England: from now on everything there would be done from the Prayer Book (amended

The Prayer Book riot

to be more high church than it was in England, to help get the Scots up to speed). Unfortunately for Charles, while Knox had been dead for more than sixty years, his spirit was alive and kicking in Scotland. In St Giles' Cathedral, Edinburgh, as soon as the newly-appointed bishop tried to read out the new Prayer Book, a member of the congregation threw her stool at him, precipitating a riot in which the bishop was lucky to get away with his life. Up in Brechin, the bishop was taking no such chances: he led the service from the new Prayer Book with a pair of loaded pistols pointed at the congregation.

The Scots gathered themselves together in a covenant (which many signed with their own blood), rejected Charles' reforms, and, when two rather reluctant armies were sent north to deal with their impertinence, they beat them both. Many across Britain now saw that here was a king ready to wage war against his people to reintroduce popish ways. He was even prepared to use an Irish Catholic army to do it. The country was soon plunged into a civil war in which Charles' army would eventually be crushed by the Puritan soldiers of a born general, the MP for Cambridge, Oliver Cromwell.

'Some new and great period'

The civil war was by no means solely about religion, but, as Cromwell himself put it: 'Religion was not the thing at first contested for, but God brought it to that issue at last.' The Puritans saw that here was a chance to achieve what they had been fighting for since Elizabeth's settlement. It was of this time that John Milton spoke when he said that 'God is decreeing to begin some new and great period in his Church, even to the reforming of the Reformation itself'. From 1643 to 1649 over a hundred Puritan theologians gathered in Westminster to write the necessary documents for the creation of a new, and properly reformed, national church. It was to be a church without bishops (archbishop

The trial of King Charles I

Laud himself was executed in 1645); it was to be a Presbyterian church (though room was made for Congregationalists like Cromwell); it was to be given a new, reformed statement of belief (the Westminster Confession of Faith), and catechisms to suit; and the *Book of Common Prayer* was replaced with the Westminster *Directory of Public Worship*.

With the execution of the king in 1649 for high treason against the people of England, the country looked very different: there was no king, there were no bishops, and the country was ruled first by Parliament and soon by Cromwell himself, as 'Lord Protector'. It was a time of unprecedented opportunity for the Puritans.

History is written by the vicars

The 1650s were not only an age of great pastoral activity by the Puritans (think of Richard Baxter's golden years in Kidderminster), they also assisted in the birth of many of their greatest scholarly achievements.

One of the foremost and most prolific Puritan scholars was an old friend of Richard Sibbes', the Primate of All Ireland, James Ussher. In the 1650s he published his *Annals of the World*, a monumental history of the world that included the notorious opening claim that the 'beginning of time, according to our chronology, happened at the start of the evening preceding the 23rd day of October (on the Julian calendar), 4004 BC' (a date immortalized in the marginal notes of the Authorized Version of the Bible for generations). However, it would be entirely unreasonable to dismiss Ussher as a naïve crackpot.

JACOBUS USSERIUS. ARCHIEPISCOPUS ARMACHANUS.

James Ussher (1581–1656)

Scholarly opinion of the seventeenth century (shared by scientists such as Kepler and Newton) was fairly happy with the idea that the date of creation could be fixed somewhere close to 4000 BC. As Professor Stephen Jay Gould of Harvard put it (while entirely disagreeing with him): 'Ussher represented the best of scholarship in his time.' It is simply that, at the time, most scholars held a different assumption to Ussher's deriders, that the Bible is a reliable source document of chronological information.

It is necessary to get past that hurdle, for Ussher was not about simply calculating the date of creation. The *Annals* are a seminal attempt at a comprehensive history of the world up to AD 70, incorporating all available historical sources. Dated such scholarship may be today, but it was of the highest order of the time, and such mighty tomes as Ussher and his academic colleagues wrote were the ripe fruit of Puritanism's 'great period'.

Something that marked out how very different the new republic (or 'Commonwealth') of England was to how things had been was its extraordinary degree of religious toleration. Now that differing openly from the old Church of England was encouraged, a whole host of different sects emerged. England became a place of 'mere Protestantism', with differences on a vast range of theological issues now acceptable. More, for the first time in nearly four hundred years, Jews were allowed back into England (the idea was that they might be converted, the conversion of Israel precipitating the Second Coming, but they were allowed to worship freely).

It did mean, however, that England in the 1650s played host to a horde of radical groups. There were the Quakers (with their emphasis on the 'inner light' as opposed to the external word); the Muggletonians (whose prophet, John Reeve, taught that Jesus alone was God, meaning that when he died on the cross, Moses and Elijah were forced to run the universe for three days); and, among others, the Ranters (for whom sin was an illusion, since 'to the pure all things are pure' [Titus 1:15]). It was the Ranters in particular, with their defence of adultery and their public displays of nudity and ecstatic blasphemy, who were so useful to the critics of the Puritan enterprise of the Commonwealth. Was this what being 'fully reformed' looked like?

The main thing, however, that began to turn people against the Puritan government was its attempt to enforce strict Christian behaviour on a nation. The theatres were closed; adultery became a capital crime; swearing (merely saying 'upon my life') could merit a hefty fine; the Sabbath was upheld (making any 'walking abroad', except going to church, illegal); and 'superstitious' holidays, such as Christmas, were abolished and replaced by monthly fast-days. When soldiers could be found patrolling London on Christmas Day, summarily inspecting houses to remove any meat being cooked, it is hardly surprising that people were put off. Ordinary citizens, regardless of their spiritual state, were being made to live as if they were 'the godly', and they could not stomach it. It was an experience that would tar Puritanism ever after in the English mind, and people began to long for the easy ways of a 'merry' government.

The merry monarch

It had not taken long before people wanted a king again. They had offered Cromwell the crown (which he had refused), and when he died in 1658, the lack of a capable successor meant they were quick to offer it to Charles, the son of the king they had executed.

Charles II, who was proclaimed king in 1660, was the very opposite of everything England had seen for the last decade. The 'merry monarch', as he became known, seemed to have as many mistresses as he had spaniels; certainly he managed to produce fourteen illegitimate children by a mere seven of them. Under the Commonwealth adultery had been a capital crime; under Charles it was chastity that was now punished – with scorn. And (dare one say it?) Charles was very cavalier about theological differences, being, if anything, a Roman Catholic at heart (certainly he converted to Roman Catholicism on his deathbed).

In this atmosphere, the reaction against Puritanism was popular and savage. In 1662 the Prayer Book was reimposed; and now, to end the arguments once and for all, the clergy were forced to declare that it contained nothing contrary to the word of God, and that as a result they would not depart from it in their churches. A fifth of them – some two thousand – refused, and were ejected from their ministries. Then, in order to prevent them from any further ministry, in 1664 the Conventicle Act outlawed religious assemblies of more than five persons outside the Church of England. The following year, the Five Mile Act prevented them from going within five miles of any 'city or town corporate or borough' where they had ministered before. Puritanism was being legally gagged.

However, Puritan ministries kept going. Some ejected clergy managed to get themselves reassigned elsewhere. Then, there were places (for example, in the Midlands, where Birmingham is today) that were more than five miles from any 'city or town corporate or borough', and these became nonconformist strong-holds. Other Puritan pastors simply braved the consequences. When, for example, in 1665 and 1666, London suffered an out-break of the plague and a city-wide fire, many of them illegally stayed with their suffering congregations to minister to them (and warn them of sin, that 'plague of plagues', and the eternal fire that must ensue). As a result of such direct flouting of the law, the persecution grew more intense, and some twenty thousand Puritans were sent to prison over the next twenty years. In Scotland they had it worse: the death penalty was imposed for such illegal preaching and torture was used liberally to hunt down suspects.

Yet, despite these late blooms on the tree of Puritanism, Charles II's regime was attacking its very roots, with withering effect. It was not just the gagging of the preachers; soon it was law that public offices could only be held by Anglicans, and that only Anglicans could go to university. It was not just that the move made the nonconformists second-class citizens, incapable of social advancement and influence; the real problem for them was that Cambridge and Oxford had been the Puritan seminaries and training-grounds. With the next generation largely barred

A man with a great burden on his back

Perhaps the most famous Puritan prisoner in the 1660s and 1670s was John Bunyan, who languished in gaol for

John Bunyan (1628–88)

some twelve years for illegal preaching. However, he managed to use his time there to conceive what is almost certainly the Puritan literary classic: *Pilgrim's Progress*. *Pilgrim's Progress* is an allegory about every Christian (journeying from the City of Destruction to the Celestial City), but it is particularly reflective of Bunyan's own experience. A tinker by trade, Bunyan was used to travelling from village to village with a 60 lb anvil and hefty toolkit on his back: it became a model for the great burden of sin his pilgrim carries on his back (until he comes to the cross and it is 'loosed from off his shoulders' to his enormous relief).

In prison, Bunyan also wrote directly of his own conversion in *Grace Abounding to the Chief of Sinners*. It gives us a highly illuminating personal example of the introspective moralism Richard Sibbes fought, and of what Bunyan found to be the answer. In it, Bunyan describes how he would despair, in his youth, when he thought of heaven and hell, believing it 'too late for me to look after heaven; for Christ would not forgive me'. When he tried to do better, he said 'my peace would be in and out, sometimes twenty times a day; comfort now, and trouble presently'.

But one day, as I was passing in the field, and that too with some dashes on my conscience, fearing lest yet all was not right, suddenly this sentence fell upon my soul, Thy righteousness is in heaven; and methought withal, I saw, with the eyes of my soul, Jesus Christ at God's right hand; there, I say, is my righteousness; so that wherever I was, or whatever I was a-doing, God could not say of me, He wants my righteousness, for that was just before Him. I also saw, moreover, that it was not my good frame of heart that made my righteousness better, nor yet my bad frame that made my righteousness worse; for my righteousness was Jesus Christ Himself, the same yesterday, and to-day, and for ever (Heb. 13.8). Now did my chains fall off my legs indeed, I was loosed from my affliction and irons, my temptations had fled away; so that, from that time, those dreadful scriptures of God left off to trouble me now; now went I also home rejoicing, for the grace and love of God.

It was this message that permeated all of Bunyan's preaching, preaching that was, apparently, of such high order that when Charles II referred to him as 'that illiterate tinker prate' in the presence of the one-time Vice-Chancellor of Oxford University, John Owen, the scholar replied 'Please, your majesty, could I possess that tinker's abilities for preaching, I would gladly relinquish all my learning'.

from any such training, the men of theological calibre died out, leaving Puritanism to be an increasingly shallow movement that would not be taken seriously again. Puritanism, after all, had been a movement concerned with words (and the word of God), and so when Puritans were no longer educated, the muscle of the movement wasted away. Worse, without strong ties to biblical moorings, over the years that followed many found themselves drifting outside belief in such Christian basics as the Trinity.

Because it died such a slow death, it is hard to say quite when the Puritan era ended. There was no final cataclysm, no last stand. There were still evangelicals in the Church of England, but so many had been ejected, gagged and suppressed that the old movement found itself ever more scattered and leaderless, until by 1700 nobody spoke much of 'Puritans' any more. By then, people spoke scornfully of 'dissenters', an ostracised, impotent, second-class group that was easily dismissed. But in another sense, if Puritanism was about 'the reforming of the Reformation', to ask when the Puritan era ended is to ask when (or if) the Reformation ended. That is the question to which we turn next.

Notes

1 Edmund Morgan, *The Puritan Family: Religion & Domestic Relations in 17th Century New England* (Harper Perennial, 1966), p. 16.

7 Is the Reformation over?

'The first and keenest subject of controversy between us'

Thus Calvin described the doctrine of justification in his response to Cardinal Sadoleto. He could not have put it more accurately, for, from the moment Luther understood from Romans 1 that God's righteousness is an entirely unmerited gift, justification was the matter of the Reformation. 'Nothing in this article can be given up or compromised,' wrote Luther, 'even if heaven and earth and things temporal should be destroyed.' It is the belief, he said, 'on which the church stands or falls'. Not everybody grasped or shared this: men like Erasmus thought reformation could be a mere moral spring-clean; radicals took it to be a simple revolt against the old ways; Zwingli just opened the Bible, but not really to find Luther's idea of justification there; and some, like Martin Bucer and Richard Baxter, understood justification differently. However, Luther's experience with Romans 1 was to be the model for the mainstream Reformation: through the Bible, the essential matter of justification was discovered. Justification was what made the Reformation the Reformation.

For those who accepted that God freely declares sinners to be righteous, justification was a doctrine of comfort and joy. As William Tyndale put it, '*Evangelion* (that we call the gospel) is a Greek word and signifieth good, merry, glad and joyful tidings, that maketh a man's heart glad and maketh him sing, dance, and leap for joy.' Luther himself felt that by it he was 'altogether born again and had entered paradise itself through open gates'. And no wonder: the fact that he, a failing sinner, was perfectly loved by God because he was clothed with the very righteousness of Christ himself gave him a dazzling confidence.

> When the devil throws our sins up to us and declares that we
> deserve death and hell, we ought to speak thus: 'I admit that
> I deserve death and hell. What of it? Does this mean that I shall
> be sentenced to eternal damnation? By no means. For I know
> One who suffered and made satisfaction in my behalf. His name
> is Jesus Christ, the Son of God. Where he is, there I shall be also.'

This happy, heartfelt reaction to justification can be sensed in the music of the Reformation. Take, for instance, the traditional

Johann Sebastian Bach

'Hosanna', sung at the Mass. In 1555, Palestrina, then almost the official musician of Rome, wrote a new score for the 'Hosanna' in his Mass for Pope Marcellus. To hear it is to hear Rome's Counter-Reformation spirituality: it is exquisite music, but there is something cerebral and dutiful about the choir's intoning of the hosannas. A hundred and ninety years later, Johann Sebastian Bach, an ardent Lutheran all the way down to his tapping toes, wrote his version of the 'Hosanna', and the difference is striking. The exact same piece was set to music, but in Bach's Lutheran hands, it has an entirely different resonance: now the hosannas are belted out with an unmistakeable, unbounded enthusiasm and joy. Such was the natural effect of believing Luther's doctrine of justification.

What, though, of those in Rome? How did they respond to Luther's teaching on justification? Given all the pyres lit and the bulls of excommunication sent, the answer might seem rather obvious. In actual fact, though, the reaction was quite mixed. For the first twenty-odd years of the Reformation there was an influential group of scholars and clerics in Italy who were reasonably sympathetic to it. One of their leading lights was a noble Venetian born in the same year as Luther, Cardinal Gasparo Contarini. Contarini had had a 'eureka' moment much like Luther's – only several years before him! On the day before Easter, 1511, he came to understand how the righteousness of Christ could be 'given and imputed unto us, as being graft into Christ, and having put on Christ'. As a result he argued that we should rely 'upon the justice of Christ given and imputed to us, and not upon the holiness and grace that is inherent in us'.

Cardinal Gasparo Contarini

However, Contarini had not read as much theology as Luther, and he failed to see the knock-on implications of his discovery for the Mass, belief in purgatory and so on. Also, with rather sweet naivety, he thought that he had merely discovered the true teaching of Roman Catholicism, and consequently never upbraided Rome, spending his life instead trying to reconcile the Roman Catholic system with his own understanding of justification.

With this belief in place, Contarini supposed that Rome and the Reformers could be reconciled quite easily. He was, then, the perfect man for the pope to send when, in 1541, a conference was arranged to meet at Regensburg, where, it was hoped, Catholics and evangelicals could end the schism. To his great delight, they did actually manage to come up with an agreed statement on justification. An amazing achievement! Sinners are justified by faith, the statement held. That satisfied the evangelicals present. However, it explained, that faith must be active in love. That satisfied the Catholics.

However, it wasn't clear: did the statement mean that only with works of love would faith attain Christ's righteousness? While Luther and Calvin were emphatic that true saving faith would always produce such works of love, they were equally emphatic that such works were the *consequence*, and not the *cause*, of justification. Making that distinction was the heart of what they fought for, and yet this statement remained ambiguous, allowing Catholics and evangelicals to read it in entirely contrary ways. The Catholic could read it as meaning that being loving is necessary for getting justified; the evangelical could read it as meaning that love is the necessary fruit of a faith which alone saves. Despite the agreed wording, then, each side meant different things by it, and thus it never amounted to a real agreement. Luther, who was not able to be present, rejected the statement as a messy patchwork of theologies (as did the pope), and snorted his frustration at its slippery language: 'The Holy Scriptures and God's commandment are by nature not ambiguous.'

The lack of consensus became increasingly clear, and the Regensburg conference soon broke down. Distraught, Contarini died under arrest the next year, his hopes of a reunion shattered as the mood in Rome quickly turned against any form of toleration for the Reformation. Four years later, in 1545, the pope

The Council of Trent

convened the Council of Trent, a great assembly of the Roman Catholic Church intended to establish her position once and for all.

From Trent, Rome's voice rang out, no longer ambiguous, but loud, clear and defiant. First, it rejected the Reformation principle of *sola scriptura* (Scripture alone), asserting that equal loyalty should be given to both Scripture (now definitively said to include the apocrypha) and to the oral traditions of what Christ and the apostles had taught concerning faith and morality. With this foundation in place, it proceeded to define justification as 'not only the remission of sins but also the sanctification and renewal of the inner man'.

It could not have been clearer: where the Reformers held justification to be a divine declaration that the sinner – while still a sinner – has been given the righteous status of Christ, Trent saw justification as the process of becoming more holy and so more personally worthy of salvation. To ensure absolutely no confusion, Trent then pronounced a string of anathemas against what it defined as heretical views on justification. For instance:

Canon 9: If anyone says that the sinner is justified by faith alone . . . let him be anathema [eternally condemned].

Canon 11: If anyone says that men are justified either solely by the imputation of Christ's righteousness or solely by the remission of sins, to the exclusion of the grace and charity which is poured into their hearts by the Holy Spirit and stays with them, or also that the grace by which we are justified is only the good will of God, let him be anathema.

Canon 12: If anyone says that justifying faith is nothing else than trust in divine mercy, which remits sins for Christ's sake . . . let him be anathema.

Canon 24: If anyone says that the righteousness received is not preserved and also not increased before God through good works, but that those works are merely the fruits and signs of justification obtained, but not the cause of the increase, let him be anathema.

Ignatius Loyola, founder of the Jesuits, the storm-troopers of the Counter-Reformation.

Unsurprisingly, from here Trent went on to affirm all the old official theology of the sacraments, purgatory, indulgences, the priesthood and so on. It also stipulated a number of practical reforms (such as having a seminary in every diocese) so that the Roman Catholic church might be a purer, stronger version of what it had always been. Encouraged by Trent, Roman Catholicism in the second half of the century enjoyed its own time of renewal:

corruption was rooted out, new and freshly devoted orders of monks and nuns were set up, and Catholic missionaries travelled to the ends of the earth. However, the days of Contarini and reconciliation were gone, and while Rome was swept clean, in her beliefs about salvation she remained as far from the Reformation as ever.

Four hundred years later . . .

At the end of the sixteenth century, every Protestant knew that the pope was the antichrist, and in Catholic regions of Europe 'Luther' was a popular name for pigs. How different things are today! Now, in the twenty-first century, Catholics and Protestants routinely cooperate, locking arms to face as one the common threats of secularism, relativism, atheism, Islam, etc. In fact, evangelicals today often find they have more in common with Roman Catholics than they do with liberal Protestants in their own denominations. More, the doctrinal retreats of Protestantism have made Rome's constancy in an age of change deeply attractive to many. Explaining why he had converted to Roman Catholicism, G. K. Chesterton wrote, 'It is the only thing that frees a man from the degrading slavery of being a child of his age.' From hurling anathemas to holding hands! No wonder the reunion of Rome and the Reformation party is now commonly seen as achievably nigh.

But how close are Roman Catholicism and evangelicalism today, really? Remarkably so, according to Professor Mark Noll and Carolyn Nystrom in their book *Is the Reformation Over?* As proof they refer to a 1996 poll taken to measure the presence of evangelicalism in Canada and the US. Respondents were marked down as evangelical if they agreed with four statements: that the Bible is 'the inspired word of God'; that 'I have committed my life to Christ and consider myself to be a converted Christian'; that 'it is important to encourage non-Christians to become

Christians'; and that 'through the life, death and resurrection of Jesus, God provided a way for the forgiveness of my sins'. On that basis, a significant percentage of Roman Catholics were labelled 'evangelical'. In fact, a quarter of these Canadian 'evangelicals' were Roman Catholic, while half of the American Catholics interviewed scored three out of four. None of this was to offend the Catholics concerned: a good number already referred to themselves as 'evangelical'.[1]

The problem with the poll, however, was that it raised none of the issues of the Reformation. In the sixteenth century, both sides of the Reformation divide (except, perhaps, for some of the radicals) would happily have agreed to those statements and found themselves labelled 'evangelical'. The inspiration of the Bible, commitment to Christ, mission, and God's provision of salvation through Jesus were never points of contention. Similarly, the cheer Noll and Nystrom display when they reveal modern Catholic-evangelical agreement over such things as the Trinity and the person of Christ seems equally misplaced. While, of course, all Christians should rejoice that there are no disagreements there, the fact is that there never were any. Agreement on such issues does not indicate that anything has changed since the Reformation.

The Reformation was, fundamentally, about justification; it was the Reformers' view of justification, as discovered in the Bible, that shaped and controlled almost every aspect of their disagreement with Rome. Thus if the Reformation is truly over, the principal reason must be that both sides have reached an agreed understanding of justification.

Noll and Nystrom argue that this has, in effect, happened, and that 'many Catholics and evangelicals now believe approximately the same thing' about justification.[2] Certainly, there is much to be said for this surprising claim. Quite apart from the wide spectrum of views held by Catholic laypeople, there are today a number of influential Catholic theologians prepared to sound remarkably like Luther on justification. For example, Father

Joseph Fitzmyer, S.J., in his commentary on Romans, denies that justification is a process of becoming more holy (the traditional Catholic view); instead, he argues, it involves the righteousness of Christ being attributed to a sinner by grace. Luther's jaw would be on the floor.

That said, there is a clear distinction in Roman Catholicism between the private views of individuals (who can fall into error) and the official view of the Church herself. The opinions of individuals are held to carry no authority in themselves, and the history of Roman Catholicism right up to the present is full of theologians being reprimanded for their views.

The question, then, is: has official Catholic teaching changed from the days of those booming anathemas at Trent? Noll and Nystrom seem positive: 'If it is true, as once was repeated frequently by Protestants conscious of their anchorage in Martin Luther or John Calvin that . . . justification is the article on which the church stands or falls . . . then the Reformation is over.'[3] Whence such confidence? On Reformation Day (31 October, when Luther nailed up his ninety-five theses) 1999, the Roman Catholic Church and the Lutheran World Federation signed the Joint Declaration on the Doctrine of Justification, claiming that 'the subscribing Lutheran churches and the Roman Catholic Church are now able to articulate a common understanding of our justification'. At this stage, Luther would be suffering a major heart attack.

And yet. Under the microscope, the Joint Declaration looks rather like the Regensburg agreement that Contarini had worked for. Just like at Regensburg, justifying faith is described as being a faith that must be active in love. And, just as at Regensburg, precisely what that means is not examined closely. On the whole, when reading the Joint Declaration, it is quite hard to know what is being said, and one gets the impression that words are being used to paper over cracks rather than give clarity. What is clear is the lack of Reformation insistence that our standing before God is not dependent on our growth in personal holiness.

Justification is described as being 'the forgiveness of sins' *and* 'liberation from the dominating power of sin'. But that is nothing like the Reformation definition of justification. Joint Declaration it may be, the curtain on the Reformation it is not.

An easier way to determine precisely what official Catholic teaching on justification is today is to look at the *Catechism of the Catholic Church*, an exposition of the Roman Catholic faith that carries the authoritative imprimatur of Pope John Paul II. This approves the Council of Trent's definition: 'Justification is not only the remission of sins, but also the sanctification and renewal of the inner man.' It then goes straight on to explain, 'Justification *detaches man from sin* which contradicts the love of God, and purifies his heart of sin.' Since by this definition justification includes our growth in holiness, the Catechism is entirely correct to conclude that we can then merit for ourselves eternal life.

With complete consistency, the Catechism also goes on to affirm belief in purgatory and indulgences, sure signs that the traditional Catholic doctrine of justification is at work. Such doctrines simply cannot be squared with a Reformational understanding of justification, for if, as Luther argued, I am given the righteous status of Christ without that status being in any way dependent upon the state of my heart or life, then there is no place for a purgatory where I am made more worthy of heaven, or indulgences to speed me there.

There has, without doubt, been something of a change in Rome, especially since the 1960s, but concerning those theological issues that caused the Reformation, no doctrine has been rescinded. Rome's view of justification remains just as it was stated at Trent, as does its belief that (as the Catechism puts it) 'Scripture and Tradition must be accepted and honored with equal sentiments of devotion and reverence.' Thus, while attempts to foster greater Christian unity must be applauded, it must also be recognized that, as things stand, the Reformation is anything but over.

'Thou hast conquered, O pale Erasmus; the world has grown grey from thy breath'

The suggestion that the issues of the Reformation might still be live sits uncomfortably with us. Most Christians today would far rather say with Samuel Johnson, 'For my part, Sir, I think all Christians, whether Papists or Protestants, agree in the essential articles, and that their differences are trivial, and rather political than religious.' And it is not just that we lament the ongoing divisions in the church; our reaction reveals something in us that is, perhaps, more important than Protestant-Catholic relations.

To modern ears, the debates of the Reformation sound like rather pernickety wars over words. Is it, we ask, really worth squabbling over whether justification is by faith (as Rome agreed) or by faith *alone* (as the Reformers insisted)? To battle over one word! Surely that can interest only those with the prickliest of doctrinal sensibilities? As for the strong language used in those debates, it just sounds shrill and unloving in our day. And to suggest that those debates are as relevant now? One might as well campaign for the reintroduction of burning at the stake, so backward and harsh does it sound.

In the twenty-first century, we do not trust 'mere' words. They are the weapons of manipulation, the tools of spin used to coerce us. We have better things to do than pick over words. We are tolerant. The spirit of the Reformation that replaced the altar with the pulpit as the focal point of each church has long gone. A pulpit? The very thought strikes us as authoritarian and manipulative. How Erasmus has conquered! As we saw in chapter 4, it was he who said, 'The sum of our religion is peace and unanimity, but these can scarcely stand unless we define as little as possible.' Simply put, we do not like theological precision, for it causes division over issues that, we feel instinctively, are not the most relevant.

Luther, of course, responded bluntly to Erasmus: 'You with your peace-loving theology. You don't care about truth.' Perhaps that was a bit harsh – and the screams of all those martyrs,

Lutheran, Calvinist, Anabaptist and Catholic, suggest to us that a little more toleration in the sixteenth century might not have been a bad thing – but they are words that capture the startling effect the Reformation has on us. For, as we look at the history of the Reformation, we are forced to ask: are there beliefs worth dying for? All those martyrs suffered for nothing if what they died for was either untrue or irrelevant. They might, of course, have been mistaken (and each side of the Reformation divide would have agreed that the other side's martyrs were mistaken), but their fates demand more than flippant dismissal.

But perhaps what is really going on is that we relegate the issues because of a submerged cultural assumption that they are not actually true. For they were hardly small concerns being debated: What will happen to me when I die? How can I know? Is justification the gift of a righteous status (by faith alone), or a process of becoming more holy (by faith)? In which case, can I confidently rely for my salvation on Christ only, or does my salvation also rest on my own holiness? Far more is at stake than a fussy concern to dot the 'i' and cross the 't' of doctrine.

What is so worrying about Erasmus' indifference to doctrine is its imprisoning and corrosive effect. Erasmus was only ever able – and only ever wanted – to sponge down the system he was in. He could take pot-shots at bad popes and wish people were more devoted, but because he was unwilling to engage with deeper, doctrinal issues, he could never bring about more than cosmetic changes. He was doomed ever to remain a prisoner of where the church was at. And so it must be in a world conquered by him. For as long as doctrine is ignored, we must remain captives of the ruling system or the spirit of the age, whatever that may be.

Having a Bible, but no gospel

Yet is all this fair to Erasmus? Was he not the one who made the Greek New Testament available, so providing the coals for the Reformation? Certainly he did, and yet his possession of the Scriptures (and his deep study of them) changed little for the man himself because of how he treated them. Burying them under convenient assertions of their vagueness, he accorded the Scriptures little practical, let alone governing, authority. The result was that, for Erasmus, the Bible was just one voice among many, and so its message could be tailored, squeezed and adjusted to fit his own vision of what Christianity was.

To break out of that suffocating scheme and achieve any substantial reformation, it took Luther's attitude, that Scripture is the only sure foundation for belief (*sola Scriptura*). The Bible had to be acknowledged as the supreme authority and allowed to contradict and overrule all other claims, or else it would itself be overruled and its message hijacked. In other words, a simple reverence for the Bible and acknowledgment that it has some authority would never have been enough to bring about the Reformation. *Sola Scriptura* was the indispensable key for change.

However, it was not just a question of the authority of the Bible; the reason Luther started the Reformation, and Erasmus did not, was the difference in what they saw as the content of the Bible. For Erasmus, the Bible was little more than a collection of moral exhortations, urging believers to be more like Christ, their example. For Luther, this was to turn the gospel on its head: its optimism displayed its utter ignorance of the seriousness of sin. As he saw it, what sinners need, first and foremost, is a saviour; and in the Bible is, first and foremost, a message of salvation. As Richard Sibbes lamented, a century after Luther, it was all too easy to lose that controlling focus on Christ and his gift of righteousness, and yet that was the very heart of true reform. For all that the Bible was opened, without the message of Christ's free gift of righteousness, there could be no Reformation.

Back to the future

The closer one looks, the clearer it becomes: the Reformation was not, principally, a negative movement, about moving away from Rome; it was a positive movement, about moving towards the gospel. Pure negative reaction was a hallmark of certain radicals, but not the mainstream Reformation. Unfortunately for us moderns, obsessed with innovation, that means we cannot simply enrol the Reformation into the cause of 'progress'. For, if anything, the Reformers were not after progress but regress: they were never mesmerized by novelty as we are, nor impatient of what was old, just because it was old; instead, their intent was to unearth original, old Christianity, a Christianity that had been buried under centuries of human tradition.

That, though, is precisely what preserves the validity of the Reformation for today. If the Reformation had been a mere reaction to a historical situation five hundred years ago, if it was just a bit of sixteenth-century 'progress', one would expect it to be over. But as a programme to move ever closer to the gospel, it cannot be.

The state of things today testifies, as loud as ever, to the need for reformation. The doctrine of justification is routinely shied away from as insignificant, wrong-headed or perplexing. Some new perspectives on what the apostle Paul meant by justification, especially when they have tended to shift the emphasis away from any need for personal conversion, have, as much as any-thing, confused people, leaving the article that Luther said cannot be given up or compromised just that – given up or compromised. And it is not just new readings of the Bible. A culture of positive thinking and self-esteem has wiped away all perceived need for the sinner to be justified. All in all, then, Luther's problem of being tortured by guilt before the divine Judge is dismissed as a sixteenth-century problem, and his solution of justification there-fore unnecessary for us today.

But it is in fact precisely into this context that Luther's solution rings out as such happy and relevant news. For, having jettisoned the idea that we might ever be guilty before God, and therefore need his justification, our culture has succumbed to the old problem of guilt in subtler ways that it has no means to answer. Today we are all bombarded with the message that we will be more loved when we make ourselves more attractive. It may not be God-related, and yet still it is a religion of works, and one that is deeply embedded. For that, the Reformation has the most sparkling good news. As Luther put it: 'sinners are attractive because they are loved; they are not loved because they are attractive.' Only this message of the counter-intuitive love of Christ offers a serious solution.

A profoundly relevant, beautiful and sweet message, a joy-giving message, a death-defying message: it is no wonder Richard Sibbes called the Reformation 'that fire which all the world shall never be able to quench'.

Notes

1 M. A. Noll and Carolyn Nystrom, *Is the Reformation Over? An Evangelical Assessment of Contemporary Roman Catholicism* (Baker and Paternoster, 2005), pp. 12–3, 23.

2 Noll and Nystrom, p. 232.

3 Noll and Nystrom, p. 232.

Reformation timeline

1304   Petrarch, 'the father of humanism', born

1305–78   Papacy moved to Avignon

1324?   John Wycliffe born

1372   Jan Hus born

1378   'Great Schism' of the papacy begins

1384   John Wycliffe dies

1414–18   Council of Constance meets to end the Great Schism

1415   Jan Hus executed on the orders of the Council of Constance

1440   Lorenzo Valla proves the Donation of Constantine to be a forgery

1450?   Johannes Gutenberg invents the printing press

1453   Constantinople, last remnant of Imperial Rome, captured by the Ottoman Turks

1466?   Erasmus of Rotterdam born

1483   Martin Luther born

1484   Huldrych Zwingli born

1492   Columbus sails to the Americas

1505   Luther becomes a monk

1509   John Calvin born in Noyon, France

1516   Erasmus publishes his Greek New Testament

1517   Luther posts his ninety-five theses to the door of the Castle Church in Wittenberg

1519?   Luther has his 'tower experience'. Zwingli begins preaching in Zurich

1520   Luther publishes his three Reformation tracts and burns the papal bull

1521   Diet of Worms. Luther taken into protective custody in Wartburg Castle, where he translates the New Testament into German. Henry VIII publishes his *Defence of the Seven Sacraments* against Luther and is awarded the title 'Defender of the Faith'

1522	Luther completes his German translation of the New Testament
1523	Zurich officially supports Zwingli's theology
1524–5	Peasants' War in Germany
1525	First adult baptisms in Zurich
1526	William Tyndale's English New Testament completed
1528	Patrick Hamilton burned for heresy in St Andrews
1529	Luther and Zwingli fail to agree on the Lord's Supper at the Marburg Colloquy
1531	Zwingli killed at the battle of Kappel. Thomas Bilney burned for heresy in Norwich
1534	Henry VIII declared 'supreme head of the church in England'. First complete edition of Luther's translation of the Bible.
1534–5	Kingdom of Münster
1536	Calvin arrives in Geneva. First edition of his *Institutes* published. Erasmus dies. William Tyndale executed. Dissolution of the English monasteries begins
1538	Calvin, expelled from Geneva, settles in Strasbourg with Bucer. The reading of the Bible in English legalized in England
1541	Evangelical and Catholic theologians meet to resolve difference at the Colloquy of Regensburg. Calvin returns to Geneva
1542	Roman Inquisition established to combat heresy
1545–63	Council of Trent
1546	Luther dies
1547	Henry VIII dies. Succeeded by his evangelical son, Edward VI
1553–8	'Bloody' Queen Mary restores Roman Catholicism to England
1558	Elizabeth I succeeds Mary, establishing a moderate Protestantism for the Church of England
1559	Calvin produces his final, definitive edition of the *Institutes*. John Knox returns to Scotland

1560   Scottish 'Reformation' Parliament makes Scotland officially Calvinist

1564   Calvin dies

1572   Thousands of French Protestants killed in the St Bartholomew's Day massacres

1576   Elizabeth I orders Archbishop Grindal to suppress the Puritan 'prophesyings'

1588   Spanish Armada fails to invade England. Scurrilous 'Marprelate' tracts appear

1593   Act Against Puritans

1603   James VI of Scotland succeeds Elizabeth I, becoming James I of England

1604   Hampton Court Conference

1605   Gunpowder Plot

1618   James I issues his *Book of Sports*

1618–19 Synod of Dordt

1620   The *Mayflower* sails from Plymouth to Massachusetts

1625   Charles I succeeds his father as king of England

1633   William Laud becomes Archbishop of Canterbury. James' *Book of Sports* re-issued

1637   Prynne, Burton and Bastwicke condemned by Star Chamber. Prayer Book riot in Edinburgh

1639   Charles I sends his first army against Scotland

1642   Civil war begins between Charles I and Parliament

1643–9 Westminster Assembly produces the Westminster Confession of Faith, two catechisms and a *Directory of Public Worship*

1649   Charles I executed. England is proclaimed a republic

1658   Oliver Cromwell, Lord Protector of England, dies

1660   Charles II proclaimed king of England

1662   A fifth of the clergy in England ejected for refusal to adhere to the Prayer Book. Persecution of the nonconformists begins

Further reading

I have marked 'must reads' with two stars.

The background to the Reformation

To get a good feel of what it was like to live in medieval Roman Catholic Europe, try S. Doran and C. Durston, *Princes, Pastors and People: The Church and Religion in England, 1500–1700* (Routledge, 1991). Or, for a bit more depth, R. N. Swanson, *Religion and Devotion in Europe c.1215–c.1515* (Cambridge University Press, 1995).

But to get inside the medieval mind, enjoy C. S. Lewis' fascinating *The Discarded Image: An Introduction to Medieval and Renaissance Literature* (Cambridge University Press, 1994).

Martin Luther

**Every Christian should read Roland Bainton's classic biography of Luther, *Here I Stand: A Life of Martin Luther* (Abingdon, 1950). A rip-roaring bedtime page-turner.

**And why not try reading some of Luther himself? You can find his great *The Freedom of a Christian* online at <http://www.theologynetwork.org/historical-theology/starting-out/the-freedom-of-the-christian.htm>. Or, if you want a bit more, Timothy Lull has gathered together an excellent little collection of Luther's more important works in his *Martin Luther's Basic Theological Writings* (Fortress, 1989).

Ulrich Zwingli and the Radical Reformers

If you want to sample the best of Zwingli, try 'On the Clarity and Certainty of the Word of God', in G. W. Bromiley (ed.), *Zwingli and Bullinger*, Library of Christian Classics (SCM, 1953).

Probably the best biography of Zwingli is G. R. Potter's *Zwingli* (Cambridge University Press, 1976).

For more on the history of the Radical Reformation, G. H. Williams has all you could need in his *The Radical Reformation* (Weidenfeld & Nicolson, 1962). Or, if you want to read the sort of things the radicals wrote, get G. H. Williams and A. M. Mergal, *Spiritual and Anabaptist Writers*, Library of Christian Classics (SCM, 1957).

John Calvin

**Calvin's *Institutes of the Christian Religion* is a must. The title makes it sound scary; inside, it is easy to read and warm in style. If you can, get F. L. Battles' two-volume translation of the 1559 edition (Westminster Press, 1960).

Otherwise, be careful what you read on Calvin: bookshops are cluttered with opinionated and biased books on him. Try anything by T. H. L. Parker, who has written well on both the man and his thought.

The Reformation in Britain

The book that has helped many see what drove the English Reformers is Bishop J. C. Ryle's classic *Five English Reformers* (Banner of Truth, 1960). Hot stuff!

To see the heartbeat of an English Reformer, have a look at John Bradford's daily prayers, online at <http://www.